STECK-VAUGHN

DEVELOPING
READING
Strategies

EDITORIAL CONSULTANTS

Mary Sue Dillingofski, Ph.D.
Reading Specialist
Educational Consultant
Chicago, Illinois

James P. Menconi
Reading Specialist
Chicago Public Schools
Chicago, Illinois

Betty Willis, Ph.D.
K-12 Reading Specialist
Cypress - Fairbanks School District
Houston, Texas

Insights

Project Design and Development: E.L. Wheetley & Associates, Inc.
Cover Design and Development: D. Childress
Cover Photography: © D. Dietrich/FPG

DEVELOPING READING STRATEGIES is a series of six
titles listed in recommended sequence:

> **Challenges**
> **Quests**
> **Ventures**
> **INSIGHTS**
> **Summits**
> **Horizons**

Published by

Printed in the United States of America.

ISBN 0-8114-5856-3

CONTENTS

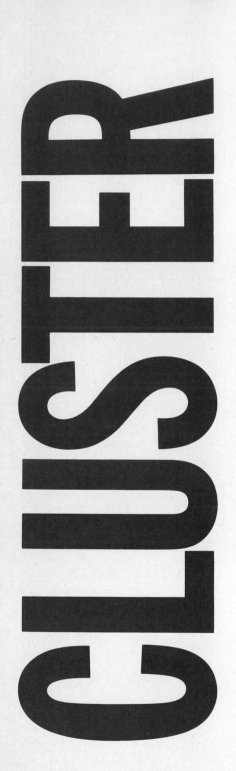

Structures

Read and learn about structures

The Great Pyramid was a memorial to King Kufu of Egypt. It took 100,000 workers almost 30 years to build. The pyramid is huge. It's made of more than two million blocks of stone, each block weighing about 2½ tons. Workers used only simple tools to move the blocks and build the pyramid. Some of the tools they used were crowbars, heavy sleds, rollers, and ramps.

The workers cut the blocks carefully. The average distance between them is only 1/50 of an inch. Workers also placed the pyramid perfectly. Its four sides line up with the true north, south, east, and west of the Earth. The size of the Great Pyramid and the way it was built make it a true wonder of the ancient world.

What do you already know about structures?

Talk about what you know. Get together with a group of students to talk about what you already know about structures. Here are some questions to help you get started:

1. What structures did prehistoric people build?
2. How did workers carve the faces of four Presidents on a mountain?
3. What buildings might people build in the future?

Write about what you know. Imagine that you were a worker who helped build a pyramid. Then picture living in the future and building a city on the moon. Which would you rather do? Give reasons for your choice. Write your answer on a separate sheet of paper.

Make predictions

Read the titles of the articles in this cluster and look at the picture on page 5. Write down three things you think you'll learn by reading these articles about structures.

1. _____

2. _____

3. _____

Start to learn new word meanings

All of the words listed below are used in the two paragraphs at the top of page 4. Study the meanings of these words as you read about structures.

ancient—of times long past. *The pyramids were built in ancient times.*

memorial—a structure created in memory of a person or event. *The statues are a memorial to our country's leaders.*

pyramid—a structure with a square base and triangular sides that meet at a point on the top. *Egyptian kings were once buried in huge pyramids.*

Learn new skills and strategies

The books you read contain much more than printed words. They also contain maps, diagrams, and pictures. You can use these pictorial aids to help understand the words you read. In this cluster, one of the skills you will learn is how to get information from pictorial aids.

Gather new information

By the end of this cluster, you will have learned the answers to these questions.

1. When did people first begin to build their homes?
2. What makes the Seven Wonders of the Ancient World so special?
3. Why was the Panama Canal built?
4. Why are the Mount Rushmore Memorial and the Watts Towers special to Americans?
5. What structures might people build on the moon?

Why People Began to Build

What do you already know?

Long ago, people did not build the structures they lived in. Write down three facts that you already know about the way early people lived. Work with a partner, if you like.

1. _____
2. _____
3. _____

Make predictions

Look at the illustrations and the words in large type in the article. Then write down three things you think you will learn about as you read this article.

1. _____
2. _____
3. _____

Set your purpose for reading

Write down one thing you hope to find out about the structures that early people built as you read this article.

_____

_____

Learn important words

Study the meanings of the words below and how they are used in sentences. Knowing these words might help you as you read this article.

prehistoric—belonging to the times before writing had been invented. *There are no written records of what life was like in prehistoric times.*

ancient—of times long past. *The pyramids were built in ancient times.*

permanent—not changing or moving. *Most prehistoric people did not live in permanent structures.*

When we think of prehistoric times, we think of men and women who lived in caves and wore animal skins. It's hard to imagine these people moving out of their caves and building homes. How did they come to make the beautiful buildings and monuments of ancient times? This change did not take place quickly. It took place over several thousand years.

Prehistoric people lived in small groups spread across the Earth. These groups had little to do with each other. But they went through the same steps as they moved from living in the wild to building houses.

Using skills and strategies

Making predictions

Predicting helps you think ahead and become ready for new ideas as you read. To make a prediction, you use the ideas you just read to figure out what kind of information will come next.

Look at the last paragraph you just read. Can you predict what the next part of the article will be about?

If you said, "how people changed from living in the wild to living in houses," you are right. Keep making new predictions as you continue to read.

How did people live long ago?

Prehistoric men and women lived in natural shelters. These shelters included caves and rocky ledges. The people lived anywhere they could because they traveled all the time. As the animals they hunted moved, so did the people. When people ate all the nuts, berries, and roots in one place, they left. As early people looked for food, they used whatever they found on the land for shelter.

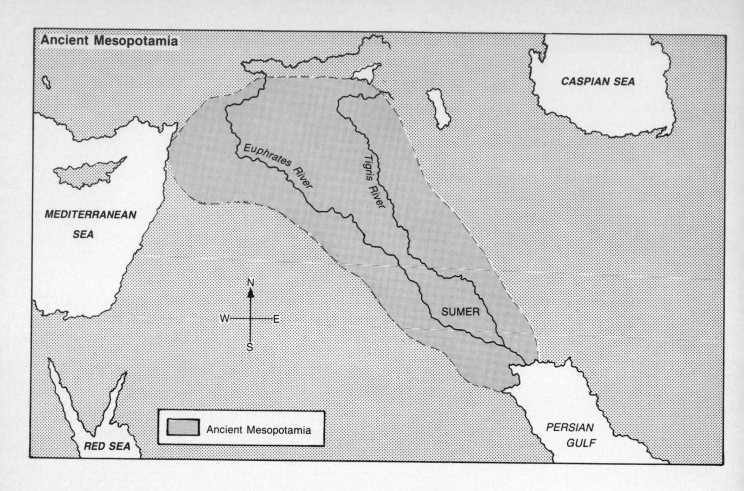

The work of finding food was hard and dangerous. Wild animals lived around them. Prehistoric people had only simple weapons made of sharpened stones or wood. Many ancient people did not live past the age of one. Most never reached thirty. They had no reason to build permanent buildings.

About 10,000 to 12,000 years ago, something happened that changed human history. Perhaps some groups learned to store extra seeds they gathered. Some of the seeds might have dropped onto the ground near where they were stored. These seeds were watered by the rain. When the people returned to eat the seeds, they would have found plants growing where none had grown before. Over time, ancient people learned how to grow plants from seeds.

Farming developed in different groups of people at different times. One of the first places farming started was in Mesopotamia. The land was perfect for growing crops. Mesopotamia had good soil and warm weather. It sits between two rivers. Look at the map above and circle the names of the two rivers.

About 12,000 years ago, barley seeds were put in the ground in Mesopotamia. They were watered by rainfall or by floods from the rivers. The seeds grew into plants. The people soon learned to become better farmers and grow more crops.

8

Using skills and strategies

Making predictions

Think about the ideas and information you just read. Can you predict how growing plants changed the way early people lived? What have you already learned that will help you make your prediction? Write your prediction in the margin.

Early farmers were the first people to live in one place. They lived near their fields. Small, wild animals also were drawn to the fields. Some of these animals, such as goats and sheep, were tamed by the farmers. Animals once chased by hunters now were being raised for food by farmers. People needed to live in caves when they moved around. Since farmers stayed in one place, they needed a different kind of shelter. Farming gave ancient people more than a food supply. It gave them a reason to build permanent homes.

Using skills and strategies

Making predictions

Was the prediction you wrote down correct? If it wasn't, think of the title of this article, "Why People Began to Build." How does this title help you predict what you will read? Write your answer in the margin above.

Read the heading in large type below. Use this to predict what you will read about next. Write your prediction in the margin below.

What were early homes made of?

Early people built their shelters from whatever was available. People who lived near trees built homes out of tree trunks and bark. Land that was full of rocks offered stones for a building material.

The homes in the drawings on page 10 were built in Mesopotamia. People built these homes using clay or reeds from the rivers. They learned to shape and bake their red clay into bricks. Other shelters were made out of river reeds covered with clay.

Bigger than a house

Farming and living in permanent homes changed the way early men and women lived. During the many years after they moved into houses, people learned how to control their water supply. They made sure their crops didn't get too much or too little water. They also developed a way to measure and count. They made tools for digging, planting, and harvesting crops. Pots were made to store grain. Writing developed.

With their new skills, people built more and larger buildings. About 1,500 years after farming began in Mesopotamia, cities began to appear. Some of the greatest cities in Mesopotamia were built by a group of people called the Sumerians. Their cities were planned around one large building, the temple. The temple was the most important building in the city. It was the home of the king and a place of worship.

The Sumerians needed great skill to build their temples. Hundreds of thousands of bricks were baked and locked together. Beautiful tiles covered the outside of the temple. Long stairs connected the different levels. These early people had begun making large and beautiful buildings.

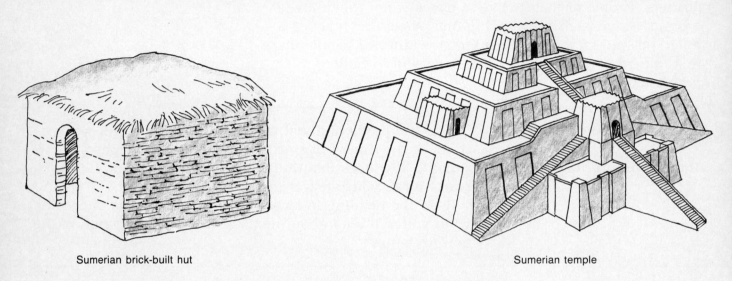

Sumerian brick-built hut   Sumerian temple

Think About What You've Read

Important ideas

1. Why didn't early people build permanent shelters?

_____

_____

2. How did farming change the course of history?

_____

_____

3. What do you think that the author meant by the heading on page 9, "Bigger than a house"?

_____

_____

_____

Use what you've learned before
4. Why did Indians who lived in forests build their homes out of logs?

_____

_____

Important word meanings
Find the words *prehistoric*, *ancient*, and *permanent* in the article. Circle the words and read how they are used. Then write your own sentences for each of the words on a separate sheet of paper.

Using skills and strategies
You made predictions before you read this article. You continued to make them as you read. What do you think helped you the most to make these predictions? Was it the title, the pictures, or the ideas you had just read? Explain your answer.

_____

_____

_____

Writing
Imagine that you were the first person to plant a seed in the ground. You watered it and discovered that it grew into a plant. This took place before writing was invented. On a sheet of paper, write a message telling about your amazing discovery without using written words.

Your important ideas
Look back over the article. Write down one idea that seems to be the most important to you—the one idea that you would like to remember.

_____

_____

Your important words
Look back at the words you have learned as you read about prehistoric people. Write down the word or words that you think are the most important—that you would like to remember.

_____

_____

The Seven Wonders of the Ancient World

What do you already know?

Write three facts that you think you already know about famous structures built by ancient people. Work with a partner, if you like.

1. _____
2. _____
3. _____

Make predictions

Preview the article by looking at the pictures and reading the headings in large type. Then write down three things you think you will learn about by reading this article.

1. _____
2. _____
3. _____

Set your purpose for reading

Write down one thing you hope to learn about the Seven Wonders of the Ancient World.

_____

_____

Learn important words

Study the meanings of the words below and how they are used in sentences. Knowing these words might help you as you read this article.

mausoleum—stone building above ground used as a tomb. *The queen was buried in a mausoleum.*

marble—a hard rock that can be made smooth and shiny. *Marble is used for statues and in buildings.*

pyramid—a structure with a square base and four triangular sides that meet at a point at the top. *Egyptian kings used to be buried in huge pyramids.*

Imagine riding a camel across the desert. Suddenly you come upon a huge stone pyramid whose base is the size of ten football fields! This is the Great Pyramid of Giza. It is one of the Seven Wonders of the Ancient World. These large and beautiful wonders were made thousands of years ago. It's hard to believe they were made by people using simple tools.

The Pyramid of Giza

Of all the wonders, only the Great Pyramid of Giza still stands today. The pyramids of Egypt were built to house the bodies of kings after they died. Nobody really knows how the Great Pyramid was built. Experts believe that over 100,000 men worked on it. The workers dragged more than two million blocks of stone to the site. They built long ramps out of dirt and brick. The stones were pulled up the ramps on sleds made out of logs.

Using skills and strategies

Pictorial Aids

Maps and pictures can help you understand the information you read in an article. Study the map of the ancient cities at the bottom of the page. It shows you where the seven wonders were located.

As you read about each wonder, circle the name of the city where it was built. Then find that city on the map. Next to each city name on the map, write the name of the ancient wonder that was built there. The Great Pyramid is already written next to Giza for you.

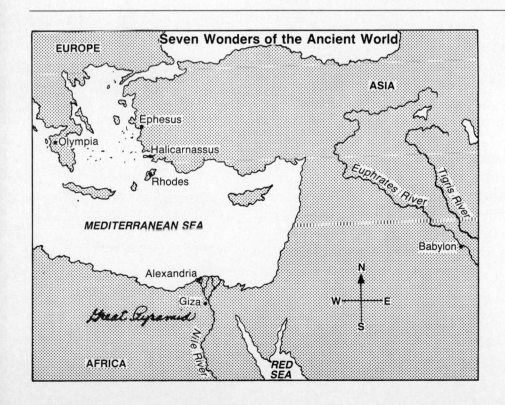

The Mausoleum at Halicarnassus

The Mausoleum at Halicarnassus was a huge gold and marble building. King Mausolus was buried there. Because this building was so beautiful, we use the word *mausoleum* today to mean a place where people are buried above the ground.

The Colossus of Rhodes

Imagine sailing on a large ship in the Mediterranean Sea. You see a statue of a man in the water, but it is twenty times larger than a man. Your boat sails between the statue's legs! This statue, called the Colossus of Rhodes, was built in honor of a battle won by the people of Rhodes. It was made of metal from the enemy's weapons.

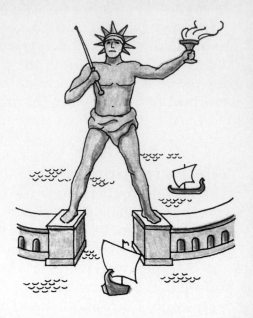

Colossus of Rhodes

The Hanging Gardens of Babylon

Long ago in Babylon, a new queen was sad about leaving her home in another country. To make her happy, the king built the most beautiful gardens ever seen. This garden of flowers and fruit trees was on top of a building 75 feet above the ground. To get water to the plants, people took turns working. They pumped water up from a river nearby.

The Statue of Zeus

The most famous statue in the ancient world was that of the god Zeus. Found in Olympia, the statue was eight times larger than a man. This wonder was made of gold and ivory. Every four years people met in Olympia to honor Zeus in contests of sport. These contests were the original Olympic Games.

The Temple of Artemis

The people of Ephesus built a white marble temple to honor the goddess Artemis. It was so large that people said it rose into the clouds. Many beautiful statues and 106 columns were part of the temple.

The Lighthouse of Alexandria

Picture yourself on a ship in a storm during the night. If you were traveling around Alexandria about 2,300 years ago, you would not worry. The 400-foot-high lighthouse would show you the way. A fire always burned at the top. The lighthouse guided ships to safety for over a thousand years.

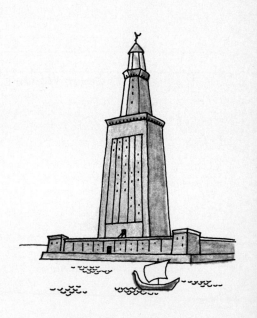

Lighthouse of Alexandria

Think About What You've Read

Important ideas
1. Why did the king of Babylon build the hanging gardens?

_____

2. How do you know that the people of Rhodes won many battles?

_____

Use what you've learned before
3. What tools could be used today to build the Great
   Pyramid? Explain why these tools would be better than
   the ancient tools.

_____

_____

Important word meanings
On a separate paper, write a short paragraph. Use all four
of these words in your paragraph: *marble*, *permanent*,
pyramid, and *ancient*. Look back at the way the words are
used in the article to be sure you use them correctly.

Using skills and strategies
Use the map on page 13 to answer these questions.

1. What two cities are found in Africa? _____

2. What city is on an island in the Mediterranean Sea?_____

3. What city is the farthest west on the map? _____

Writing
You plan to make a statue of a famous person. On a sheet
of paper, write some notes telling where the statue will be
placed, what it will look like, and what it will be made of.
Include a simple drawing of your statue in your plans.

Your important ideas
Look back over the article. Write down one idea that
seems to be the most important one to you—the one idea
that you would like to remember.

_____

Your important words
Look back at the words you have learned as you read
about the Seven Wonders of the Ancient World. Write down
the word or words that you think are most important—that
you would like to remember.

_____

Building the Panama Canal

What do you already know?
With a partner, write down three facts that you already know about the Panama Canal.

1. _____
2. _____
3. _____

Make predictions
Look at the pictures and the headings in large type in the article. Then write down three things that you think you will learn as you read this article.

1. _____
2. _____
3. _____

Set your purpose for reading
Write down one thing that you hope to find out about the Panama Canal as you read this article.

_____

_____

Learn important words
Study the meanings of the words below and how they are used in sentences. Knowing these words might help you as you read this article.

excavate—to remove dirt and rock from an area. *Workers had to excavate tons of dirt to make the Panama Canal.*

lock—a part of a canal in which the level of the water can be changed. *Letting water into the lock raises the ship.*

engineering—the design and making of buildings and systems. *Engineering is a good career for people who like building.*

Since the 1500s, many countries wished for a canal across Central America. It would link the Atlantic and Pacific oceans. Ships would no longer need to make the long and hard trip around South America. In 1903, the United States signed a treaty with Panama to build a canal for all nations. The treaty gave the United States control of a canal zone ten miles wide.

Using skills and strategies

Pictorial Aids

Maps often give you information that is not in the text. For example, the map on this page helps you understand distances that are not described in the article. Find New York City on the map. Circle the number of miles you would travel if you went from New York City to San Francisco using the Panama Canal. Now circle the number of miles you'd travel going around the tip of South America. How many miles are saved by using the canal? Write this information in the margin next to the map.

Preparing to build a canal

Before work could begin on the canal, engineers had to overcome two big problems. The first was disease. Malaria and yellow fever were common. These diseases were spread by mosquitoes. Because of the hot, wet climate, there were many mosquitoes in Panama. To control them, workers drained the swamps and cut down tall grasses. They also built water systems so canal workers would have pure water to drink. By the end of 1905, yellow fever was wiped out. Fewer people died from malaria.

The second problem was transportation. Workers had to remove rocks and dirt that they excavated from the canal. The workers and their supplies also had to be carried to the work sites. Engineers solved this problem with a two-line railroad. It ran the 50-mile length of the canal.

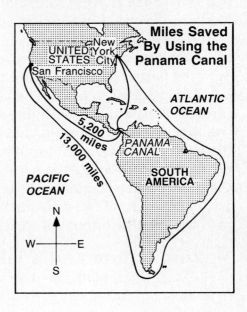

Building the canal

President Theodore Roosevelt and Congress approved the canal in 1906. It would include locks, a lake, and a dam. These things had been built before but never on such a large scale.

Cutting through a mountain. The hardest part of building the canal was digging an eight-mile passage through a small mountain. Workers used over 33 million pounds of dynamite to dig this passage. Dynamite loosened the dirt and rocks. Then steam shovels loaded the dirt and rocks into railroad cars. In all, 96 million cubic yards of dirt and rock were removed from the mountain.

Much of the work on the Panama Canal was done by hand. Workers excavated tons of dirt with shovels.

Panama was a dangerous place to work. Dynamite blasts killed many workers. Others were killed or hurt by machines. There were landslides. A landslide could kill workers and wipe out months of work in a minute.

Building the locks.   While other work was going on, the areas for the locks were excavated. Locks were needed because parts of the canal are higher than the ocean. Six pairs of locks were built. This allowed ships to travel through the canal in both directions at once.

About 4.5 million cubic yards of concrete were poured for the locks. Railroad cars brought huge buckets of concrete to the site. Cranes and cables lifted the buckets and poured the concrete for the locks. Gates were added that would open and close to let ships in and out of the locks. Each gate weighed hundreds of tons.

Making a dam and a lake

The engineers' plan called for building a dam across a nearby river that often flooded. Dirt and rock from excavating the mountain were used to build the dam. When the river was dammed up, it no longer flowed into the Atlantic Ocean. Instead the water formed a lake 24 miles across.

How the locks work

The lake is higher than the oceans on both sides. The locks are arranged like steps from the lake to the oceans. Gates between locks allow the water in each step to be at a different level. Huge tunnels carry water into or out of a lock at the rate of 26 million gallons in eight minutes. This allows the lock engineers to raise or lower the water level in each lock. A ship will enter a lock and be carried up or down to the level of the next lock, from ocean to lake and from lake to ocean.

Using skills and strategies

Using Pictorial Aids

Write in the margin how a ship is raised or lowered by going through the locks. Use the photo below and the information in the text to help you.

When the first ship went through the Panama Canal on August 15, 1914, the locks worked perfectly. The many problems had been overcome by one of the world's greatest engineering jobs. When the work was finished, workers had built the world's largest earthen dam. They had made the world's biggest man-made lake, and the canal's locks were the largest in the world. Engineers today still are amazed at the work done to build the Panama Canal.

The completed Panama Canal is an engineering wonder. Ships are able to move through the canal in both directions.

Think About What You've Read

Important ideas

1. How were yellow fever and malaria kept under control?

_____

_____

2. What was the hardest part of building the canal?

_____

3. Why did engineers build a two-line railroad instead of a single track?

_____

_____

4. Why couldn't the people who built the pyramids have built the Panama Canal?

_____

_____

_____

Important word meanings

On a sheet of paper, make up a sentence using each of these words: *engineering, excavate, lock, prehistoric,* and *permanent.* Instead of writing the words in the sentences, write them at the bottom of the paper. Leave a space in each sentence where the missing word belongs. Check your paper to be sure only one of the words makes sense in each sentence. Give your paper to a classmate and see if your classmate can fill in the correct answers.

Using skills and strategies

Write a caption for the picture on page 18. Why do you think landslides would be especially unwelcomed by the workers?

_____

_____

_____

Writing

Imagine that you are in charge of finding people to build the Panama Canal. On a sheet of paper, write an ad for people to apply for jobs. Be sure to name the jobs that must be filled.

Your important ideas

Look back over the article. Write down one idea that seems to be the most important one to you—the one idea that you would like to remember.

_____

Your important words

Look back at the words you have learned as you read about the Panama Canal. Write down the word or words that you think are most important—that you would like to remember.

_____

Gifts to Their Country

What do you already know?

With a partner, write down three facts that you think you know about Mount Rushmore or the Watts Towers.

1. _____

2. _____

3. _____

Make predictions

Look at the pictures and the headings in the article. Then write three things you think you will learn about as you read this article.

1. _____

2. _____

3. _____

Set your purpose for reading

Write down one thing you hope to learn about Mount Rushmore or the Watts Towers as you read this article.

_____

_____

Learn important words

Study the meanings of the words below and how they are used in sentences. Knowing these words might help you as you read the article.

immigrant—a person who leaves a country to live permanently in another country. *The immigrants from Italy settled in New York City.*

memorial—a monument created in memory of a person or event. *The statue is a fitting memorial for the town's leader.*

sculpture—a work of art made by carving materials or putting hard materials together. *The Watts Towers is a huge piece of sculpture.*

People sometimes say that good things come in small packages. But Gutzon Borglum and Simon Rodia didn't agree. Both men were immigrants to the United States. Each gave a large and lasting gift to his new country.

Gutzon Borglum and American art

High atop a cliff in the Black Hills of South Dakota, four faces are carved into Mount Rushmore. The faces of George Washington, Thomas Jefferson, Abraham Lincoln, and Theodore Roosevelt are about 60 feet high. They overlook the canyon below. However, some people say they really are watching over the future of our country.

Each of these men served as President during a critical time in this nation's history. Washington was the first President of the country. Jefferson wrote the Declaration of Independence. Lincoln kept the country together during the Civil War. Roosevelt was the President who led the building of the Panama Canal. Borglum wanted the memorial to stand for the spirit of America. He was proud of the ideals of Americans.

Using skills and strategies

Self-questioning

People often ask themselves questions about the things they read. Asking themselves questions helps them keep the things they have read straight in their mind. It also helps them recognize important information when it occurs later. For example, as you read the paragraphs above, you might have asked yourself:
1. Who were Gutzon Borglum and Simon Rodia?
2. How did faces of presidents get carved into a mountain?

You can find some information to answer the first question in the paragraphs above. However, you will have to continue reading to find out about the second question.

As you continue reading, ask yourself questions about the most important ideas. Write your questions in the margin. Leave room under your questions to write answers later.

The idea for a memorial in the Black Hills first came from other people. However, it was Gutzon Borglum who made the idea real. Borglum planned the memorial himself and directed most of the work.

Borglum's family came to the United States from Denmark. From childhood, Borglum showed great promise as an artist. He believed that art in America should be about America. It should remember American achievements. He also believed that art should last. Borglum said that sculptures should be "cut into the crust of this Earth."

Gutzon Borglum, right, rides up the face of Mount Rushmore to view his giant sculpture.

Using skills and strategies   Did you write any questions in the margin? If you didn't,
think about what you read and write some questions now.
Self-questioning   Continue to write your own questions in the margin.

The carving of Mount Rushmore

Carving the faces involved two main steps. First, the rock
was excavated with dynamite to create the general shape of
each face. Large pieces of rock were blasted off at exact
places. Then the faces were carved on the mountain.
Workers used drills and jackhammers as carving tools.

Borglum's workers had a hard job. They hung from the
side of a stone cliff at the top of a mountain. They had to
learn to handle heavy tools and keep their balance at the
same time.

Mount Rushmore is much larger than most sculptures.
The faces are as high as a six-story building. Borglum
created a grand monument to the country he loved.

Using skills and strategies

Self-questioning

Did you ask yourself questions about the way the Mount Rushmore Memorial was made?

The next section is about a different artist and a different work of art. Your questions might be like the ones you asked about Borglum and Mount Rushmore. Write the questions you ask yourself in the margin.

Simon Rodia and the Watts Towers

"I'm going to do something for the U.S.A. before I die—something big." This was the promise of an immigrant named Simon Rodia to his new country. Like Gutzon Borglum, Rodia wanted to create a work of art as a gift to the United States. The result was the largest structure that one man ever made all by himself.

Rodia was born in Italy in 1879. Brought to the United States at the age of ten, he worked as a logger, miner, and builder. Rodia finally settled in Watts, a part of Los Angeles. He became a tile salesman.

In 1921, Rodia began building something in his yard in Watts. He used pieces of steel pipe, bed frames, tiles, broken bottles, and shells. He searched city dumps and beaches for odds and ends to add to his work. Soon he had three towers. Rodia worked alone for 33 years. He asked no one for money or advice.

24

Today Rodia's towers sparkle under the sun or the moon. They are shaped like cones, rising 100 feet from a concrete base. The base itself sparkles as passing lights catch the colorful pieces of glass and tile buried in it.

Many smaller towers form the three tall towers. In fact, all the towers are made up of a system of walls, arches, and sculptures. This is Simon Rodia's work of art. This is his gift to the country that welcomed him many years before.

Many people saw the Watts Towers as a new kind of American folk art. (His art was new to America and the world.) Rodia's towers acted as a model for the many young artists who saw or heard about them. However, some people thought that the towers were unsafe. They wanted them torn down.

In 1954, Rodia decided that his work was finished. He was tired. He also was angry because some people didn't like his towers. Rodia gave his house, his land, and the towers to a neighbor. Then he moved away to another part of California. Rodia died fifteen years later at the age of ninety. He never returned to view his gift.

Both Simon Rodia and Gutzon Borglum wished to make something lasting to honor their country. They created two very different works of art. Each is a gift of the artist's love for America and its people.

Think About What You've Read

Important ideas

1. What common goal did Gutzon Borglum and Simon Rodia share?

_____

_____

2. What idea did Borglum want Mount Rushmore to stand for?

_____

3. Why do you think that some of Simon Rodia's neighbors thought his towers were unsafe?

_____

_____

Use what you've learned before

4. How were the building of the Panama Canal and the Mount Rushmore Memorial alike?

_____

_____

Important word meanings

Circle a sentence in the article where each of the words below is used. Then write your own sentences using each of the words.

immigrant   excavate   sculpture   memorial

_____

_____

_____

_____

Using skills and strategies

Go back to the questions you wrote as you read this article. Write the answers to your questions in the margin by each question. If you can't answer a question, write down what information you would need to give an answer. Sometime soon, visit a library and look for the answers to your questions.

Writing

Have you ever worked on something important for a long time only to have someone else not like it? On a separate sheet of paper, write a paragraph telling what happened.

Have you ever not liked something that was important to someone else? Write a second paragraph telling what happened.

Your important ideas

Look back over the article. Write down one idea that seems to be the most important one to you—the one idea that you would like to remember.

_____

_____

Your important words

Look back at the words you have learned as you read about the Watts Towers and Mount Rushmore. Write down the word or words that you think are most important—that you would like to remember.

_____

_____

Living on the Moon

What do you already know about the moon?
Write down three facts that you already know about the moon. Work with a partner, if you like.

1. _____

2. _____

3. _____

Make predictions
Look at the pictures in the article. Then write down three things you think you will learn by reading about living on the moon.

1. _____

2. _____

3. _____

Set your purpose for reading
Write down one thing that you hope to find out about living on the moon as you read this article.

_____

_____

Learn important words
Study the meanings of the words below and how they are used in sentences. Knowing these words might help you as you read this article.

gravity—the force that draws smaller objects to a larger object. *The moon is held in orbit by Earth's gravity.*

lunar—relating to the moon. *Work on a lunar base could begin in the year 2000.*

orbit—to travel in a path around a body in space. *Some day there may be a space station in orbit around the moon.*

radiation—rays of heat, light, or other energy, such as those from the sun; some rays are dangerous. *Much of the sun's radiation reaches the moon because the moon has no air.*

When you see science fiction movies, you often see strange-looking buildings. They may be on the moon or on planets. Some are underground. Others hang in midair. These buildings are imaginary. But one day they might really exist. People will live on the moon in special buildings that protect them from radiation, extreme heat or cold, and other dangers.

What buildings will be on the moon?

Writers have imagined a below-ground lunar city. It is covered with a clear dome filled with air. There are shades, or giant blinds, outside the dome. These shades protect people from the sun's radiation. Writers made up these ideas. However, the ideas are very close to the truth. Many scientists believe that a city on the moon must be below ground level and covered with a dome.

Using skills and strategies

Thinking about what you already know

You usually know some things about articles, even before you begin reading. You can use what you already know to help you better understand the things you read. For example, you know that every space suit has a helmet. Space suits have helmets because there is no air to breathe in space.

Underline the sentence that tells you that the dome of a lunar city will be filled with air. How can you use what you already know to understand why a dome must be built over the city? Write your answer in the margin.

A spacesuit allows astronauts to breathe and walk in space. Without the suit, the effects of radiation and lack of air would harm the astronaut.

One building would be very important in a lunar city—a laboratory for scientific research. In it, scientists would study such things as the effects of low gravity on people and animals. Telescopes would be set up to look out on planets and stars. Scientists also would study the moon's crust. Spacecraft could use the moon as a base for exploring planets in the solar system. The moon laboratory would help scientists make great progress in their research.

Using skills and strategies

Thinking about what you already know

You have probably seen movies of American astronauts hopping around on the surface of the moon. Do you remember why they were hopping, not walking?

Underline the sentence above that says scientists on the moon would study the effects of low gravity on people and animals. Why do you think scientists can study the effects of low gravity on the moon? Write your answer in the margin.

Exploring on the moon

Scientists and engineers hope that a moon base will be built in the near future. Work may start around the year 2000 and be completed in the year 2007. That will be fifty years after the first man-made object was put in orbit around the Earth.

A space station will be built first so that space crews can live and work in orbit longer than is now possible. This space station will have a living area for the crew and enough food and water for a year. People will live in this space station until a permanent one is built on the moon.

Living on the moon

Living on the moon will be hard. Growing food on the moon will be a big problem for people living there. Water and air will have to be made on the moon. Plant food will have to be added to the soil. Scientists will have to develop special crops that can grow on the moon.

People also will have to get used to the different time cycle on the moon. The moon does not rotate. The same side always faces the Earth. However, as the moon travels around the Earth, its two sides take turns facing the sun. All places on the moon have two straight weeks of sunlight and two weeks of darkness.

People living on the moon certainly would be on a very different world. But it will be like the United States in one important way. The people will probably come from many countries. They will bring different kinds of knowledge, skills, and customs to their new world. Someday, in the near future, this may really happen.

Think About What You've Read

Important Ideas
1. Why would a moon base probably be built underground?

_____

_____

2. Name three problems people living on the moon would have.

_____

_____

_____

Use what you've learned before
3. Is building a lunar city as important as building the Panama Canal? Explain your answer.

_____

_____

30

Important word meanings

Go back to the article and underline the sentences where the words *gravity, lunar, orbit,* and *radiation* are used. Write a sentence using one of these words on the line below.

_____

Write a sentence that tells how the word *immigrant* could refer to the people who settle the moon.

_____

Write a sentence using the word *engineering* that tells why building a moon base would be an engineering triumph.

_____

Using skills and strategies

Find a part of the article where you used something you already knew to understand what you read. In the margin, write what you already knew. Then underline the sentences you understood because of this information.

Writing

Imagine that the lunar city has been built and you are living on the moon. You are writing a TV show about life on the moon to show on Earth. What would you show in your opening scene? Look back over the article and choose what you think would make the most interesting beginning. Write your opening scene on a separate sheet of paper.

Your important ideas

Look back over the article. Write down one idea that seems to be the most important one to you—the one idea that you would like to remember.

_____

_____

Your important words

Look back at the words you have learned as you read about cities on the moon. Write down the word or words that you think are most important—that you would like to remember.

_____

_____

Reviewing What You Have Learned

Some facts and ideas you have learned

You learned many important facts and ideas as you read about structures. A few of them are listed below. On another sheet of paper, write your own list of important ideas. You can look back at the "Your important ideas" section of each lesson to remember the ideas you wrote down.

- People began to build their homes about 10,000 years ago when they began farming.
- The Seven Wonders of the Ancient World were very large and they were made by people using simple tools.
- The Panama Canal made travel between the Atlantic and Pacific oceans much easier.
- The Mount Rushmore Memorial and Watts Towers were gifts from immigrants who loved their country.
- People soon might build a city on the moon.

Some word meanings you have learned

Here are some of the important words you learned in the articles you read. Make sure you understand their meanings. Then add important words of your own. You can look back at the "Your important words" section of each lesson to remember the words you wrote down.

permanent—not changing or moving. *Most prehistoric people did not live in permanent structures.*

lock—a part of a canal where the level of the water can be changed. *Letting water into the lock raises the ship.*

engineering—the design and making of buildings and systems. *Engineering is a good career for people who like building.*

_____

_____

_____

_____

_____

Purposes for reading

Look back at the section at the beginning of every lesson called "Set your purpose for reading." What purposes did you set for reading the articles in this cluster? Write down one or two of your purposes and how the information in the article helped you achieve that purpose. Write your answer on another sheet of paper.

Using skills and strategies

Choose one article in this cluster. Find two places where you used something you already knew to understand what you read. Write down what you already knew. Then tell how you used your own ideas to help you understand the information you read.

_____

_____

_____

_____

Writing: personal opinion

The articles in this cluster describe things people have built over thousands of years. Which structure would you most like to visit? Write a paragraph that tells why you want to visit this structure. Explain your reasons. For example, if you want to visit the structure because of its beauty, describe how it is beautiful. Share your paragraph with your class.

Revising

Read what you wrote. Can you think of any important reasons for visiting the structure that you might have left out? Go back to your paragraph and add these reasons.

Activities

1. Make a time line for the ancient world. Look up *man* in an encyclopedia. Find out when people first appeared on Earth. Begin your time line at that date. Using equal distances and equal numbers of years between dates, draw a time line. Add the events you think are important, such as the first appearance of people, the beginning of farming, and the invention of writing.
2. Look up *Stonehenge*, a structure built by prehistoric people in England. Find out how it compares to the Seven Wonders of the Ancient World. Report what you learn to the class. Use a map or a picture to help you present your report.
3. Look for information about famous artists who were immigrants to the United States. Find examples of their art and share them with your classmates.

Deserts

Read and learn about deserts

A group of adults and children travel down a dusty road. Some of them lead skinny goats. Others ride slowly along the arid road on camels. The animals travel from one side of the road to the other, looking for something green to eat.

A child at the front of this group of wandering nomads spots tall palm trees in the distance. She yells that an oasis is near. Suddenly, the entire group of animals and people begins to move quickly, hurrying to reach their goal. At the oasis, the animals will have grass to graze on and water to drink. The people will be able to bathe and eat a good meal. However, the nomads will not stay at the oasis for very long. They will soon load their camels and move their goats to the next oasis in the desert.

What do you already know about deserts?

Talk about what you know. Get together with other students to talk about what you already know about deserts. Here are some questions to help you get started:

1. What plants and animals live in the desert?
2. How is it possible to live and work in the desert?
3. What can people do to make changes in the desert?

Write about what you know. Pretend that you are going to visit a place in the desert. Name three items that you think you should take with you on your trip. Then list the items. Put the most important item first. Put the least important item last.

_____

_____

Make predictions

Read the titles of the articles in this cluster and look at the picture on page 35. Write down three things that you think you'll learn by reading these articles about deserts.

1. _____

2. _____

3. _____

Start to learn new word meanings

All the words listed below are used in the two paragraphs at the top of page 34. Study the meanings of these words as you read about deserts.

arid—too dry for things to grow. *The farmer could not grow any crops on his arid land.*

nomad—a person with no fixed place to live. *The nomad carried goods through the desert on his camel.*

oasis—an area in a desert where water is found. *The date palms are one kind of tree that grows in an oasis.*

Learn new skills and strategies

One of the strategies you will learn about in this cluster is summarizing. People summarize when they remember in their own words the things they have learned. Learning how to summarize can help you remember important ideas or study for a test.

Gather new information

By the end of this cluster, you will have learned the answers to these questions.

1. Where is the world's largest desert located?
2. How does a cactus plant store water?
3. What desert battle was a turning point of World War II?
4. In what type of houses do the Indians of the desert live?
5. How do people plan to use icebergs from the North and South poles to change the deserts?

Deserts of the World

What do you already know?

Write down three facts that you already know about the world's deserts. Work with a partner, if you like.

1. _____

2. _____

3. _____

Make predictions

Look at the pictures and headings in the article. Then write down three things that you think you will learn as you read this article.

1. _____

2. _____

3. _____

Set your purpose for reading

Write down one thing you hope to find out about the world's deserts as you read this article.

_____

_____

Learn important words

Study the meanings of the words below and how they are used in sentences. Knowing these words might help you as you read this article.

Equator—an imaginary line around the Earth, midway between the North and South poles. *The weather is usually hot near the Equator.*

water vapor—water in the form of a gas. *When water boils, it changes from a liquid to water vapor.*

current—a flow of water or a running stream. *The wind blowing across an ocean current can warm a coast or keep it cool.*

Many people think of a cartoon when they think of a desert. In the cartoon, the sun beats down on a man. The man is crawling through hot sand in search of water.

The cartoon is close to the truth. In real deserts, the air temperature is often 120°F, and the ground is usually 30–50°F hotter than the air! Winds blow the hot air around. There is little or no rain. In fact, a desert gets less than 10 inches of rain a year. What little rain does fall is quickly dried up by the heat and the wind.

Only a few kinds of plants can grow in the desert. Yet, the desert's bare ground can be beautiful. Would the place in the picture be any more beautiful if the ground were covered with grass and trees?

Using skills and strategies

Summarizing

A summary is a short statement of important ideas. For example, you wouldn't tell a friend all that you saw and heard at a movie. You would summarize—briefly tell about the important parts of—the movie. You might retell the movie in your own words.

Summarizing is a good way to help you remember the important ideas in something you read. Here's a summary of the last two paragraphs you just read:

Deserts get less than 10 inches of rain each year. They're very hot during the daytime and usually windy. However, deserts can be very beautiful.

As you read the next two paragraphs, notice that the sentences that help you answer the question in the heading are underlined. Marking the important ideas in your text will help you summarize later.

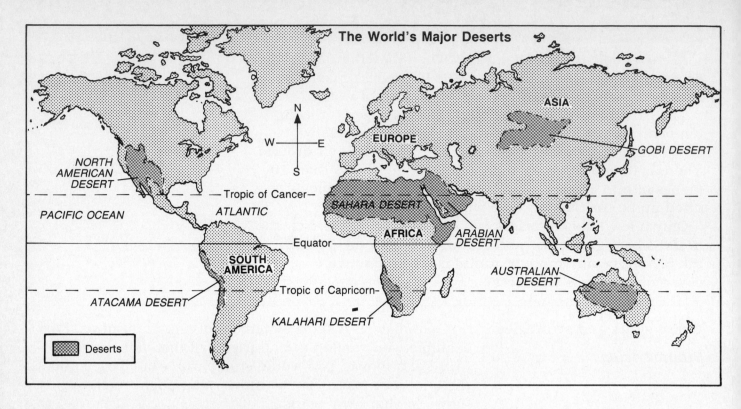

The World's Major Deserts

Where are deserts located?

You probably do not live in a desert. Most people live where the weather is wetter, cooler, and less harsh. But almost every continent has deserts. The map above shows where the world's deserts are located. Notice first that there are no deserts at the far north or far south of the Earth. Now find the Equator on the map. This imaginary line divides the Earth into two parts called the Northern Hemisphere and the Southern Hemisphere. Draw along the Equator with your pencil. Are deserts found along the Equator? You're right if you said no.

Look north and south of the Equator. Most deserts in the world lie in two bands north and south of the Equator. The deserts lie on either side of the lines of latitude called the Tropic of Cancer and the Tropic of Capricorn. You might shade in these areas on the map with your pencil to help you remember where the deserts are.

What causes a desert?

You know that clouds are formed when water vapor in the air cools and forms tiny drops of water. When the drops become too heavy to stay in the air, the water falls to the ground as rain.

Take away the clouds that cover an area and, in time, you'll have a desert. The sun's heat will dry up all the water that is on the ground and the soil will turn to dust. Of course, no one has taken away the clouds over the deserts. There are other reasons it doesn't rain in the deserts of the world.

Read the next section to find some reasons, or causes, to explain why deserts are dry. Circle them as you read.

When you finish reading, write a summary of the causes that explain why deserts are dry. Write your summary in the white space in the margin of this page. Remember to use your own words in the summary.

The winds that blow over some deserts, such as the North American Desert and the Sahara, are dry. They have already dropped the water vapor they picked up over the oceans. As they blow over the desert, these winds help dry up any drops of water that might be on the ground.

Rivers of ocean water called currents flow along coasts. When these currents are cold, the winds blowing over them turn cold. Cold winds cannot carry much water vapor. So the land next to the coast is dry. This is why the Atacama Desert is so dry. It hardly ever rains there. In fact, some parts of the Atacama Desert haven't had any rain for more than two hundred years!

Some deserts are just too far from the ocean, so winds blowing over them lose water vapor before they get to them. The winds that blow over the Gobi Desert and parts of the Sahara have already gone many miles. They have lost most of the water they picked up over the oceans.

Mountains sometimes get in the way and keep some areas from getting rain. The picture shows what happens when winds coming from the Pacific Ocean meet the Sierra Nevada Mountains in North America. The winds cool as they go up the mountains, causing it to rain on that side of the mountain. The rain makes the San Joaquin Valley lush and green. The winds blowing over the mountains are dry. On the other side of the mountains is the hottest part of the North American Desert—Death Valley.

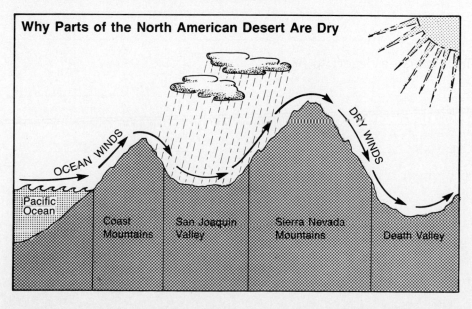

Why Parts of the North American Desert Are Dry

OCEAN WINDS

DRY WINDS

Pacific Ocean

Coast Mountains

San Joaquin Valley

Sierra Nevada Mountains

Death Valley

Famous desert facts

Just for your information, here are some facts you may or may not know about the deserts of the world.

- The Sahara is the biggest desert of all. It covers 3½ million square miles of Africa. This is about as large as the fifty states. The Sahara has mountains, and it even has a lake the size of New Jersey.
- The highest recorded temperature ever is 136°F. Of course, that was in the shade!
- The Arabian Desert is the world's sandiest desert. Almost one-third of the Arabian Desert is sand.
- Underground springs pop up and form oases in certain places in the deserts of Africa and Arabia. Palm trees and other small plants grow here. People farm and graze animals in the oases around these springs.
- Snow sometimes falls in the winter on high deserts or deserts that are far from the Equator. Snow has even fallen in Death Valley.

Think About What You've Read

Important ideas

1. How much rain falls in a desert?

_____

2. Name the desert on the continent where you live.

_____

_____

3. What are two ways that winds cause a desert to be dry?

_____

_____

_____

4. How could a very dry place be near a place that gets a lot of rain? Give an example.

_____

_____

_____

5. What kind of ocean current—cold or warm—runs near the east coast of the United States? Explain.

_____

_____

_____

Important word meanings

Underline the sentences on pages 38 and 39 where *Equator*, *water vapor*, and *current* are used. Then write a sentence of your own for each of the three words.

_____

_____

_____

Using skills and strategies

On the lines below, write down some of the important ideas in the article. Be careful to pick the most important information and state it in your own words. When you finish, you will have written a summary of the article.

_____

_____

_____

Writing

Think back about the cartoon described in the first paragraph of the article. On a separate sheet of paper, draw a cartoon of a thirsty person in the desert. Then write a caption for that cartoon. Use words that fit the way the desert probably makes you feel.

Your important ideas

Look back over the article. Write down one idea that seems to be the most important one to you—the one idea that you would like to remember.

_____

Your important words

Look back at the words you have learned as you read about the deserts of the world. Write down the word or words that you think are most important—those that you would like to remember.

_____

Plants and Animals of the Desert

What do you already know?

Write two things that you already know about the plants and animals of the desert. Work with a partner, if you like.

1. _____

2. _____

_____

Make predictions

Look at the pictures on pages 43, 44, and 45 of the article. Then write two facts that you think you will learn as you read this article.

1. _____

2. _____

Set your purpose for reading

Write down one or two things you want to learn about plants and animals of the desert as you read this article.

_____

_____

Learn important words

Study the meanings of the words below and how they are used in sentences. Knowing these words might help you as you read this article.

arid—too dry for things to grow. *Rain can turn the arid desert soil into a garden.*

moisture—small drops of water or other liquid in the air or on a surface. *The man wiped the moisture from his head as he walked through the desert.*

nectar—a sweet liquid made by plants and sometimes eaten by animals. *The bees used the flowers' nectar to make honey.*

burrow—a hole or tunnel in the ground made by a small animal. *The ground squirrel stores nuts in its burrow.*

Each day the hot sun bakes the arid desert soil. If rain does fall during the year, it runs off the hard ground barely sinking in. Yet many kinds of plants and animals live in the desert. How do they find food, water, and protection?

Desert plants hold moisture

Many desert plants grow quickly when moisture is in the ground. The plants' seeds are protected by hard outer coverings and can lie in the arid soil for years. When rain falls, the coverings break open and new plants spring to life.

When the flowers dry out, their seeds fall to the ground. Some are eaten by hungry animals. Others lie buried in the soil, waiting for another heavy rain to start the cycle again.

Not all desert plants grow fast and then disappear. Some, like the cactus, live for many years. The cactus can live in the desert because it doesn't need much water. A cactus plant has many roots near the top of the soil to get the water it needs from even a light rain. During a rainstorm, the roots may collect enough water to last the plant a year. The stems and branches of the cactus stretch like a balloon to hold the water.

Using skills and strategies

Using Pictorial Aids

The pictures and drawings in a book can help you understand the information you read in an article. One way you can use pictures is to compare what you see in the picture with what you read. Here is an example.

Look at the underlined sentence in the paragraph you just read. It explains why cactus roots are near the soil's surface. Now, look at the drawing. It gives you some information about cactus roots that the text does not. It shows you that cactus roots extend in a wide area around the plant. How does this help explain why the cactus can collect a lot of water in a short time? Write your answer in the margin.

Desert plants make other life on the desert possible. Tiny animals make their homes in the plants and in the shade they give. When plants bloom, birds, bats, and insects eat the nectar in the flowers. As the flowers dry up, some plants make a fruit to hold their seeds. Small animals often eat the fruit and scatter the seeds on the ground.

Desert animals drink little or no water

All desert animals have one thing in common. They must be able to survive without having to drink very much water.

Using skills and strategies

Using Pictorial Aids

Look at the picture of each kind of animal as you read about that animal. Find one detail in each picture that is not described in the article. Describe the detail you found by writing in the margin below.

Scorpion   Gila monster   Roadrunner

Insects. Most animals in the desert are insects. Ants, beetles, wasps, bees, flies, locusts, and many other insects live in the desert. They get the water they need from moisture that plants give off. In turn, the juicy insects are eaten by spiders, bats, birds, and reptiles.

Reptiles. Lizards, snakes, tortoises, and other reptiles live in the desert. A reptile's body temperature is always about the same as the temperature around it. So a reptile must stay in the shade or bury itself underground during the hottest part of the day and the coldest part of the night. The shell of the tortoise and the scaly skins of other reptiles help keep moisture inside their bodies. A tortoise can go for six months without drinking any water.

Birds. Because their normal body temperature is about 106°F, birds can stand higher temperatures than reptiles or mammals. However, they must protect their eggs from the broiling rays of the sun, or the eggs will cook. Desert birds find whatever shelter they can during the heat of the day and pant rapidly to keep cool.

Mammals. All desert mammals try to avoid the sun. Rats and other seed-eating rodents live in burrows, where it is cooler. They pile up seeds in their burrows and plug up the entrances to their burrows. A few desert animals, such as the kangaroo rat, make their own water from seeds they eat. The kangaroo rat never drinks any water during its lifetime.

The camel, which lives in the Sahara and Arabian deserts, is the largest desert animal. It stores fat in its hump when food is plentiful. When it is not, the camel lives off the fat. The camel also can store a large amount of water throughout its body. This allows it to go without drinking water longer than other mammals can.

The camel uses very little water for cooling its body. It can let its body temperature reach 106°F. When the camel's body temperature rises during the day, it stores up heat. During the night, it uses the stored heat to keep warm. By morning its temperature might drop as low as 94°F.

Think About What You've Read

Important ideas
1. How does a cactus plant collect and store water?

_____

_____

2. How do plants help the desert animals?

_____

_____

3. Compare the ways that a reptile and a camel control their body temperatures.

_____

_____

4. Why would animals that sweat a lot have trouble living in the desert?

_____

_____

Use what you've learned before
5. Name three of the deserts where the plants and animals described in this article live.

_____

Important word meanings

Each word in dark type is followed by two pairs of words with different meanings. Underline one word in each pair that gives a clue about the meaning of the word in dark type. The first two pairs of words are underlined for you.

current	<u>moving</u> or still	land or <u>water</u>
nectar	sweet or sour	liquid or solid
burrow	under or above	bright or dark
arid	green or brown	mud or dust
Equator	real or imaginary	middle or top
moisture	sun or clouds	damp or dry

Using skills and strategies

Look at the picture of the camel on page 45. Write one idea you can see in the picture of a camel that isn't described in the article.

_____

_____

_____

Writing

Imagine that you are a scientist who has just spent time studying animals in the desert. Write some notes for a report. Tell about two or three things that you saw and what time of day these events happened. Use a separate sheet of paper.

Your important ideas

Look back over the article. Write down one idea that seems to be the most important one to you—the one idea that you would like to remember.

_____

_____

Your important words

Look back at the words you have learned as you read about desert plants and animals. Write down the word or words that you think are most important—those that you would like to remember.

_____

_____

Desert Battles of World War II

What do you already know?

Write down three facts that you think you know about World War II or the battles that were fought in that war. Work with a partner, if you like.

1. _____

2. _____

3. _____

Make predictions

Look at the pictures and quickly skim the article. Then write down three ideas that you think you will learn as you read this article.

1. _____

2. _____

3. _____

Set your purpose for reading

Write down one thing that you hope to find out about desert fighting in World War II as you read this article.

_____

Learn important words

Study the meanings of the words below and how they are used in sentences. Knowing these words might help you as you read this article.

mirage—an effect that takes place on a sea or desert that causes distant objects to look upside down, float, or appear closer; also can be something unreal. *The thirsty man found out that the lake was a mirage.*

barren—not producing very much plant life. *The lack of rain caused the farm to become a barren field.*

radiator—a series of thin metal tubes used for cooling a hot liquid. *The truck overheated because its radiator leaked.*

Many countries fought in World War II. This war, which took place between 1939 and 1945, divided the countries of the world into two sides. One side was called the Allies, and the other side was called the Axis. The United States, Britain, Russia, and several other countries made up the Allies. Germany, Japan, and Italy were the main countries of the Axis.

Great battles took place in many different kinds of places during World War II. Men fought in the snow and cold of Russia. Battles also were fought in the hot, wet rain forests of Southeast Asia and on tiny islands in the Pacific Ocean. One of the most important battlegrounds of the war, however, was the arid African desert.

Fighting in the desert

Soldiers often said that the desert was probably a good place for a war—that is, if you really had to fight one. During a war, soldiers live outdoors all the time. The warm weather and dryness of the desert were better than the rain, snow, or mud of other places.

Of course, hot, dry weather wasn't always such a good thing. Temperatures of 120°F were common. Sand and dust got into everything. During battles, the dust thrown up into the air by tanks, trucks, and shells was as thick as fog. The wind also stirred up great storms of sand and dust almost every day. The desert winds were strongest in the late afternoon, right after the hottest part of the day. The dirt and heat caused both men and machines to break down. However, most fighters in World War II agreed that heat and dirt were better than freezing cold and mud.

To soldiers, the oddest thing about the desert was its emptiness. Nothing might be seen for hundreds of miles— no houses, no roads, no trees. Strange sights called mirages seemed to grow from the empty sands. Mirages took the form of imaginary lakes. Or else distant objects—unreal and real—appeared to float and move about in space. The soldiers often feared they might become completely lost in this barren land. They worried that they might wander right into the enemy camp. Even worse, they might just disappear in the desert and die of thirst, never to be seen again.

The desert fighters developed their own special way of dressing during the war. Most men wore only the clothing that was necessary. It was not unusual for soldiers to wear only shorts and boots. Sometimes, the only sign of an officer's rank was drawn in pencil across his shoulders.

Water, of course, was the most valuable thing in the desert. Each man normally got one gallon of water a day to serve all his needs. These needs included washing, cooking,

The hot sun and barren land of the desert made fighting battles tough on the soldiers and equipment.

and drinking. The same water also was put into the radiators of tanks, cars, and trucks to keep them from overheating. A careful man might be able to use only one quart of water for both washing and cooling his vehicle. In the morning he would carefully pour his water into a can and use the water for washing. At night he would skim the soap suds off the water and use it for washing a second time. The next morning, the man would pour the water into the radiator of his vehicle.

Preparing for the big battle

Many people think that the most important battle of World War II took place in 1942 on the barren desert of North Africa. The Battle of el Alamein, as this battle was called, marked the turning point of the war.

Using skills and strategies

Sequences

Many articles are arranged in the order in which events took place. As you read these articles, you learn what happened first, what happened next, and so on. The order in which the events took place is called the sequence. The next two paragraphs tell you what was happening in World War II before the Battle of el Alamein.

Before the Battle of el Alamein, the United States and the Allies seemed to be losing the war. Germany controlled most of Europe. German troops were more than a thousand miles inside Russia, and German bombs fell nightly on Britain. The Japanese controlled China and Southeast Asia. Much of the American navy had been destroyed in a surprise attack by the Japanese. Axis submarines controlled the oceans, destroying many supply ships every day.

The Allies were losing the desert war too. German and Italian tanks were charging toward the biggest prize of all, the Suez Canal. If the Axis conquered the Suez Canal, they could control the entire coast around the Mediterranean Sea. The Axis might then control all the Middle East and Asia too.

Using skills and strategies

Sequences

The rest of this article tells you about the events that took place in the Battle of el Alamein. The order of these events is made clear because many sentences have words that help you understand sequence.

As you read the rest of this article, underline any words that help you understand the sequence of events. These words are underlined for you in the next two paragraphs.

The Axis soldiers were led by General Erwin Rommel who was known as the "Desert Fox." Rommel began his march toward the Suez Canal in May, 1942. The Desert Fox was certain that he would win. He boasted, "Look, there's a city. I'm going to take it. There's a pass. I'll take that, too. There's Cairo, I'll take that. And there—there is the Suez Canal. I'm taking that as well." On June 29, 1942, Rommel's desert army was within one victory of reaching its goal.

No place to retreat

The Allied commanders let their soldiers know that there would be no more retreating and no giving up. The Allies could not allow the Axis to take the canal. A heated battle began on June 30 at el Alamein. The powerful Axis army, however, could not defeat the Allied soldiers. In two weeks of fighting, Rommel's soldiers could not advance. In fact,

The Battle of el Alamein in North Africa was a turning point of World War II. Tanks led Allied soldiers in their defeat of the Axis army.

the Allies began to do some attacking themselves. By mid-July, the Desert Fox called off his troops and began planning a second attack. However, he never had a chance to carry out his plans.

In August the Allies named General Bernard Montgomery to head their desert army. Montgomery spent the months of August and September increasing the size of the Allied forces. By early October, 1942, Allied soldiers outnumbered the Axis soldiers 230,000 to 80,000.

Montgomery led the Allied forces in a huge attack that began on October 23, 1942. Rommel's desert army was defeated in only a few weeks. By early November, the Axis had retreated into a small part of the desert. The Axis continued to fight on for almost two more years. However, they never again staged a major attack. It was only a matter of time before the Allies drove the Axis out of Africa.

Winston Churchill, the British leader, summed up the importance of the desert battle this way. "Before Alamein, we never had a victory. After Alamein, we never had a defeat."

Think About What You've Read

Important ideas

1. What names were given to the two groups of countries that fought in World War II?

2. Why did soldiers like the desert better than other places to fight a war?

3. Why do you think that Rommel was known as the "Desert Fox"?

Use what you've learned before

4. What was the name of the desert where the Battle of el Alamein took place?

5. What do you think the author meant when he said that the heat and dust often caused men to break down?

Important word meanings

Go back to the article and circle the sentences where the words *mirage*, *radiator*, and *barren* are used. Write a sentence using one of these words on the lines below.

_____

_____

Circle any other words in the article whose meanings you may not know. Choose one of these words and write it below. Then look in a dictionary to find the meaning of the word you chose. Write a sentence that uses the word.

_____

_____

Using skills and strategies

Tell the sequence of the following events by numbering them from 1 to 6. Use the words you underlined in the article to help you.

_____ **a.** The Allies name Montgomery to lead their army.

_____ **b.** Rommel's army is within one victory of winning the canal.

_____ **c.** The Allies build up the size of their forces.

_____ **d.** The Axis army is defeated.

_____ **e.** Rommel begins planning a second attack.

_____ **f.** The Axis army begins its march toward the Suez Canal.

Writing

Imagine that you are a soldier fighting in the desert. On a separate sheet of paper, write a letter to a friend at home. Give details about life in the desert.

Your important ideas

Look back over the article. Write down one idea that seems to be the most important one to you—the one idea that you would like to remember.

_____

_____

Your important words

Look back at the words you have learned as you read about the desert battles of World War II. Write down the word or words that you think are most important—those that you would like to remember.

_____

_____

Living and Working in the Desert

What do you already know?
Write down two problems that people who live and work in the desert must overcome. Work with a partner, if you like.

1. _____
2. _____
_____

Make predictions
Look at the pictures in the article. Then write down three things you think you will learn by reading "Living and Working in the Desert."

1. _____
2. _____
3. _____

Set your purpose for reading
Write down one idea that you would really like to learn about people who live and work in the desert.

_____

Learn important words
Study the meanings of the words below and how they are used in sentences. Knowing these words might help you as you read this article.

adobe—a building material made of sun-dried earth and straw. *Bricks made of adobe are baked in the desert sun.*

nomad—a person or tribe with no fixed place to live. *The nomad moved constantly in search of water and food for her goats.*

oasis—a fertile area in a desert where fresh water is found. *People who live in the desert travel to an oasis for food and water.*

pueblo—an Indian village in New Mexico or Arizona made of flat-roofed houses that are connected together. *Indians still live in the Taos pueblo.*

Deserts are a hard place for people to live. The lack of water makes growing plants or raising animals difficult. Yet people have lived and worked in deserts for all history. Two deserts where people live are the huge Sahara Desert and the North American Desert. The people who live in these deserts are half a world apart. However, many of the ways that they live are surprisingly alike. Go back to the map on page 38 and circle the Sahara and North American deserts.

Using skills and strategies

*Thinking About
What You Already Know*

You probably know some things about most subjects, even before you begin reading about them. You can use what you already know to help you better understand the things you read.

For example, go back and read what you wrote about the problems faced by people in the desert. You chose these problems because you already have some ideas how people might live and work in the desert. Before you read the next section, think about what you already know about a desert oasis. Write one of these facts you already know in the margin.

The oasis dwellers of the Sahara

The Sahara has no rivers. However, springs rise to the surface from underground streams in many places. Wells are sunk to get water from the underground streams in other spots. If they have water, people in the desert can grow crops. They can raise animals and let them graze on grass. They can make a green island in the desert. These green islands are called oases.

Life on an oasis is quite like life in a small farming town. Most people are farmers. They grow such crops as dates, figs, wheat, rice, and beans. Other people work in shops or cafes, or they run small businesses. Oases are sometimes busy places because land traffic through the Sahara always goes through these green islands of the desert.

The nomads of the Sahara

In the past, most of the people who lived in the desert didn't stay in a fixed place. They were nomads, or wanderers. Many different groups of nomads lived in the Sahara. The Tuaregs are the best known of the nomads. The Tuaregs wear flowing robes and ride camels. They are the desert people most often shown in movies about the Sahara Desert.

You already have some ideas about how nomads live in the desert. Your ideas may have come from sources such as movies, books, or pictures. However, no matter where you got your ideas, you can use what you already know to help you understand new ideas that you read.

Write down three facts you already know about desert nomads in the margin of your book. If you find a sentence in the next section that has the same idea you wrote down, circle that sentence.

The Tuaregs and the other groups of nomads had three main ways of making a living. The first way was carrying and selling goods. They raised camels which carried loads thousands of miles across the desert. The nomads bought and sold such products as food, salt, and gold.

The second way that desert nomads made a living was by raising animals. They moved from oasis to oasis with herds of grazing animals such as goats. The animals supplied the nomads with milk, cheese, and meat.

A few nomads made a living in a third way: they were raiders. Raiding nomads would steal food from farmers in the oases. They also would sweep down on desert traders carrying goods and demand payment to let the traders pass.

Nomads don't make a living by stealing each other's goods any more. Carrying goods also isn't as important as it once was. The airplane and special desert trucks move goods more quickly and cheaply than camels can. However, nomads still lead their herds of animals from oasis to oasis in search of grazing land.

North American desert groups

American Indians in the North America Desert lived very much like groups in the Sahara. Some Indians farmed in places where water was found. Other Indians were nomads. They moved herds of animals across the desert in search of grass or else raided the homes of other Indians.

The Pueblo Indians

Some Indians of the American Southwest created towns called pueblos. They built these towns at places in the desert where they found water. Like the desert groups of the Sahara, the Pueblo Indians were made up of several different groups whose ways of life were not exactly the same.

The Indians of the pueblos grew as much of their food as possible. Maize (Indian corn), beans, and pumpkins were among crops usually grown at the pueblos. They hunted for meat, and they tamed animals to raise for food. Wild turkeys were one kind of animal tamed by the Pueblo Indians. The Pueblo Indians also made jewelry, pots, and baskets. The jewelry, pots, and baskets they made were often used to trade at other pueblos. They traded for things they needed or wanted and could not make themselves.

The Pueblo Indians built large towns. Their pueblo houses are built like apartment houses with the living areas connected together. The houses are built of stone or adobe, and are sometimes four or five stories high. Two of these houses can be found in the pueblo in Pecos, New Mexico. One has 585 rooms and the other has 517 rooms!

Many Pueblo Indians still live and work in the deserts. In New Mexico, nineteen pueblo cities are still being lived in. Although the insides of the pueblo houses have been made more modern, they are much the same as they were before the United States was founded. Two buildings of one of the pueblos at Taos, New Mexico, are over eight hundred years old. They were built three hundred years before Columbus sailed to the Americas.

Like the oasis dwellers of the Sahara, the Pueblo Indians sometimes traded with and were often raided by the nomads of the American desert.

Nomads of the American desert

One group of American Indian nomads was the Apaches. They lived in houses that could be taken apart easily and carried along in their search for food. The Apaches, who usually lived by hunting animals, came to the desert from the grassland areas to the east. Over time, they drifted into the lands of the Pueblo Indians. Since the Pueblo Indians were successful farmers, they usually had food stored up. This made the Pueblo Indians targets for raids by the nomadic Apaches.

Today, the nomads of the American Southwest, the Apaches, have stopped wandering. They have become expert farmers and ranchers. The Apaches also have learned the ways of the business world. They have produced motion pictures that are filmed on their land. Another group operates a ski resort in the mountains above the desert.

Think About What You've Read

Important ideas

1. In what parts of the Sahara Desert do people raise crops?

_____

2. Name three ways the nomads of the Sahara once made a living.

_____

3. How were the Pueblo Indians and the oasis dwellers alike?

_____

Use what you've learned before

4. Why did the Tuaregs use camels instead of other animals to carry their goods across the desert?

_____

Important word meanings

Fill the blanks in the sentences with one of the words below. Then write your own sentence using the vocabulary word. Use each word only once.

pueblo	**nomad**	**water vapor**
adobe	**oasis**	**mirage**

1. The water of the _____ can make the desert green.

_____

2. The Indians made _____ bricks out of mud and straw.

_____

3. The lake I thought I saw was only a _____ .

_____

4. The _____ had houses with flat roofs and many rooms.

_____

5. A cloud of _____ rose from the boiling water.

_____

6. A _____ wanders from place to place in the desert.

_____

Using skills and strategies

Read the titles listed below. Next to each title, name an article that you have already read that gives facts on the same subject.

1. "The Secrets of Desert Plants" _____

2. "The People of the Gobi Desert" _____

3. "Weather of the Atacama Desert" _____

Writing

Imagine you are a desert nomad who goes from oasis to oasis trading goods. Write a short letter to a person in the United States. Tell that person what goods you trade. Also write about the people you meet on your travels. Write your letter on another sheet of paper.

Your important ideas

Look back over the article. Write down one idea that seems to be the most important one to you—the one idea that you would like to remember.

_____

_____

Your important words

Look back at the words you have learned as you read about living and working in the desert. Write down the word or words that you think are most important—that you would like to remember.

_____

_____

Deserts of the Future

What do you already know?

In many parts of the world, plans are being made to make desert lands more useful for people. Write a fact that you know which tells how desert lands can be made more useful. Work with a partner, if you like.

_____

_____

_____

Make predictions

Look at the pictures and read the headings in large type in the article. Then write down three ideas that you think you will learn about by reading "Deserts of the Future."

1. _____

2. _____

3. _____

Set your purpose for reading

Write down one or two things that you hope to learn about future deserts by reading this article.

_____

_____

Learn important words

Study the meanings of the words below and how they are used in sentences. Knowing these words might help you as you read this article.

desalination—the removal of salt from seawater. _Seawater can be made into drinking water by desalination._

reclaim—bring back to a useful condition. _Plans are being made to reclaim desert lands._

transform—to change the condition of something. _Water can transform the desert from arid land to farmland._

About 20 percent of the Earth's land is desert. This arid land receives less than 10 inches of rain each year. Another 15 percent of the earth's land is semi-arid, or almost desert. It gets from 10 to 18 inches of rain in a year. The semi-arid land could lose its ability to grow plants if rainfall amounts change. This could bring the total amount of desert in the world to 35 percent.

Deserts are wastelands. They can't be used for farming unless ways can be found to bring water to them. Therefore, they can't help feed the growing number of people in the world. However, if deserts can be watered, they can become gardens where people gladly will live. Bringing water to deserts is a problem that is being attacked by scientists all over the world.

Reclaiming the desert

Irrigation is a fairly simple way of watering the deserts in some areas. If a lake or a river is close to a desert area, water can be brought to the desert through canals. For example, water from the Colorado River irrigates farmland in southern California. This farmland was once desert land. The water from the Colorado River helped reclaim this land from the desert.

Using skills and strategies

Making Predictions

When you read, you often make predictions about what you will read next. Making predictions is a way of thinking ahead. You can better understand the things that you read if you take the time to think ahead.

You made three predictions before you started reading this article. Would you change any of your predictions now that you've read the first part of this article? If you think you can make a better prediction, write it in the margin.

Bringing fresh water through canals is probably the easiest way to irrigate a desert. It's harder when there is no fresh water nearby.

Desalination

Many of the world's deserts are close to oceans. The water in the ocean contains salt. Salt water cannot be used to drink or water crops. However, if the salt is removed from the water, it can be used. Removing salt from seawater is called desalination and can be done in several different ways.

Using skills and strategies

Making Predictions

The underlined sentence that you just read should help you predict what you will read next. Write that prediction in the margin of your book.

Large quantities of water are needed for the irrigation of deserts. A nearby river or lake is needed to supply the fresh water.

One way that salt is taken from seawater is by the greenhouse method. Look at the picture that shows this method as you read how it works. In the greenhouse method, salt water is pumped into a glass building. The sun heats the water and it turns to water vapor. The water vapor rises to the ceiling where it forms into drops. Since the ceiling is sloped, the water runs down the sides of the building into containers. The water vapor that rises from the seawater contains no salt. Therefore, the water that collects in the containers also has no salt. This water can be pumped out and used for drinking or for irrigation.

The same idea can be carried out without the greenhouse building. Any method of heating seawater and collecting the salt-free water vapor will work. Most desalination methods are based on the same idea: boil salt water and collect the salt-free water.

Greenhouse Method

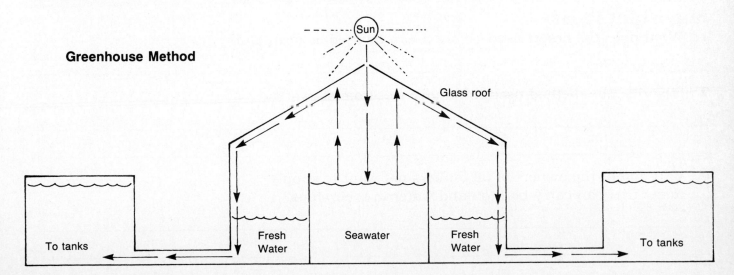

Oil and water

Desalination and irrigation are not the only ways to bring fresh water to dry areas. One way to supply water for the deserts is to use huge oil tankers. Many desert countries, such as those in the Arabian Desert, are oil rich but water poor. Oil tankers have very big tanks for holding the oil while it is moved to other countries for sale. The tankers unload the oil and return empty to the desert to take on more oil. If these ships had tanks that could be cleaned, they could bring fresh water back to the desert. Of course, it would cost a lot to put tanks in oil tankers that could be cleaned well enough to carry water.

Icebergs in the desert

More than 75 percent of the world's supply of fresh water is ice. This water is in the great sheets of ice that cover the North and South poles. One interesting suggestion for bringing water to the deserts calls for using this ice.

Using skills and strategies

Making Predictions

You have already read most of this article. Therefore, you have a great deal of information that you can use to make a prediction about what you will read next. Write this prediction in the margin of your book.

The great icebergs in the ocean contain no salt. They could be towed to desert countries. There they would be chopped up and stored in giant ice houses. The ice would melt and could be used as needed. Scientists estimate that only about 10 percent of each iceberg would melt during towing if it were covered with plastic.

Think About What You've Read

Important ideas

1. What does the desert need before it can be used as farmland?

---

2. Describe one method used to remove salt from seawater.

---

3. Why might the owners of oil tankers not want to supply tanks that can carry both oil and water in their ships?

Use what you've learned before
4. How is desalination similar to the way that rain clouds form?

_____

_____

Important word meanings
   Circle a sentence in the article where each of the words below is used. Then write your own sentences using three of the words.

reclaim	transform	desalination
arid	water vapor	

_____

_____

_____

Skills and strategies
   Look back at the predictions you wrote down while reading "Deserts of the Future." Give one reason why you made each of these predictions.

_____

_____

_____

Writing
   Imagine you have opened a new iceberg-towing business. On a separate sheet of paper, write a short ad for your company explaining what your company does and why desert countries should use your towing service. Remember to give your company a name.

Your important ideas
   Look back over the article. Write down one idea that you would most like to remember.

_____

_____

Your important words
   Look back at the words you have learned as you read about future deserts. Write down the word or words that you think are most important—those that you would like to remember.

_____

_____

Reviewing What You Have Learned

Some facts and ideas you have learned

You learned many important facts and ideas as you read about deserts. A few of them are listed below. Add your own important ideas to the end of this list. You can look back at the "Your important ideas" section of each lesson to remember the ideas you wrote down.

- The Sahara Desert has about the same area as the fifty United States.
- The stems and branches of a cactus can hold enough water to last the plant one year.
- The Battle of el Alamein in the North African desert was a turning point of World War II.
- Some Indian groups in the North American Desert lived in pueblos that had over two hundred rooms.
- The fresh water trapped in icebergs someday might be used to water the deserts.

_____

_____

_____

_____

_____

Some word meanings you have learned

Here are some of the important words you learned in the articles you read. Make sure you understand their meanings. Then add important words of your own. You can look back at the "Your important words" section of each lesson to remember the words you wrote down.

moisture—small drops of water or other liquid in the air or on a surface. _The man wiped the moisture from his head as he walked through the desert._

mirage—an effect that takes place on a sea or desert that causes distant objects to look upside down, float, or appear closer; also can be something unreal. _The thirsty man ran toward the lake, but he found that it was a mirage._

adobe—a building material made of sun-dried earth and straw. _Bricks made of adobe are baked in the hot desert sun._

_____

_____

_____

Purposes for reading

Look back at the section at the beginning of every lesson called "Set your purpose for reading." What purposes did you set for reading the articles in this cluster? Choose one of your purposes. Tell how your purpose was met or plan a way to meet your purpose.

Using skills and strategies—summarizing

Read the paragraph below. Then write a short summary of its main idea on a separate sheet of paper.

None of the men who fought in World War II were happy about being shot at. However, the soldiers who fought in the desert were glad about one thing—few people lived there. When planes dropped bombs, the bombs never killed a child. When tanks roared forward, they never crushed a farmer's crops. When the big guns threw shells toward the enemy, the shells never landed in some unlucky person's house. One soldier even suggested a new law—all future wars have to be fought in the desert!

Writing: personal opinion

You learned many facts about the desert as you read the articles in this cluster. Some of these facts might make you want to visit the desert. Other facts might make you want to stay away. On a separate sheet of paper, write a short essay for your friends. Tell whether you think the desert would be a good place or a bad place to visit.

Revising

Go back and read what you have written about visiting the desert. Did you leave out any reasons for your opinion? If so, add these reasons to your essay.

Activities

1. Go to the library and find information about surviving in the desert. Then prepare a short talk on the subject for your class. Make sure that you include information about what to do if you get lost.
2. Look at the pictures in *Drylands: The Deserts of North America* by Philip Hyde (San Diego: Harcourt, Brace, Jovanovich, 1987). This book contains many photos of the North American desert. You will be amazed at the variety of desert landscapes.
3. Plan a visit to a natural history museum in your city or a city near your home. When you visit the museum, plan to see the exhibit on the American Indians who live in the desert.

Food

Read and learn about food

We eat and drink because food provides what our cells need to grow and to give off energy—so we can work and play. Even though people can go a long time without eating, they will not live long without water. Water is so important that it is called a nutrient, something that nourishes the body.

The picture shows some of the foods you can buy at almost any grocery store. Which of these foods do you eat every day?

What do you already know about food?

Talk about what you know.   Get together with a group of students to talk about what you already know about food. Here are some questions to get you started.

1. Are there some people who hunt or find all the food they eat? How do they do this?
2. What happens to food after you eat it?
3. Do some people have emotional problems about food?

Write about what you know.   On a piece of paper, list all the foods you ate yesterday or another day you can remember. Look at your list. What ways can you think of to group the foods? Rewrite your list on the lines below, putting the foods in the groups you thought of.

_____

_____

_____

_____

Make predictions

Read the titles of the articles in this cluster and look at the pictures. Write down three things you expect to learn by reading these articles about food.

1. _____

2. _____

3. _____

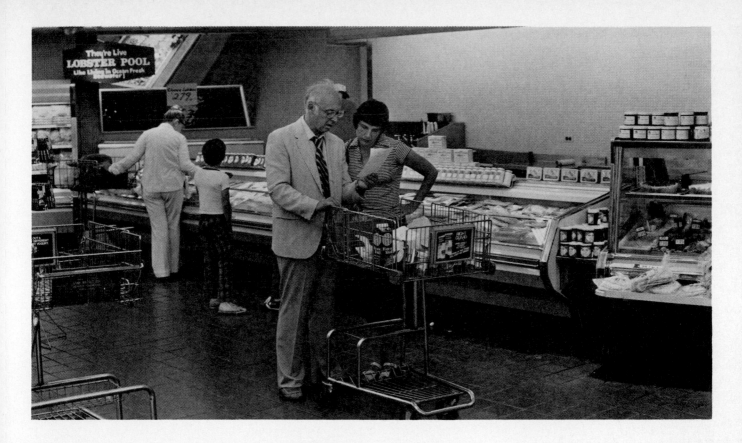

Start to learn new word meanings

All of the words listed below are used in the two paragraphs at the top of page 66. Study the meanings of these words as you read about food.

cell—the basic unit of living matter of which all plants and animals are made. *All the cells in your body need food to grow and carry on their work.*

energy—the power to work or act. *Your body uses energy when you work, play, and even when you sleep.*

nutrient—a substance the body needs to grow and stay healthy. *Proteins are an important nutrient.*

Learn new skills and strategies

One of the strategies you will learn about in this cluster is using a dictionary. A dictionary can give you information on what a word means and how the word is used. Other skills and strategies you will learn about are main idea and visualizing.

Gather new information

By the end of this cluster, you will have learned the answers to these questions.

1. How did people thousands of years ago get their food?
2. Where does digestion start?
3. What does a food preparation worker do?
4. Why do people sometimes eat too much or not enough when they are unhappy?

People Who Live Off the Land

What do you already know?

Write down three facts that you already know about what it means to live off the land and who the groups of people might be. If you like, work with a partner.

1. _____

2. _____

3. _____

Make predictions

Look at the pictures in this article. Read the headings. Then write down three facts that you think you will learn as you read this article.

1. _____

2. _____

3. _____

Set your purpose for reading

Write down one thing you hope to find out about people who live off the land as you read.

_____

_____

Learn important words

Study the meanings of the words below and how they are used in sentences. Knowing these words might help you as you read this article.

aborigine—a person who is the first to live in a place. *Indians are aborigines of North America.*

ancestor—a person who lived a long time ago in your family. *All of my ancestors came from Australia.*

caribou—the reindeer of North America. *Herds of caribou roam the cold lands of North America.*

The pictures on this page show two ways people today get their food. People get food in many ways. In our country and in most countries of the world, people buy food in stores. Some people grow some of the food they eat. They also might raise animals such as chickens for food. Many people eat meals in restaurants.

You know that people were not always able to get food in stores or restaurants. The aborigines, or the first people in every place, used whatever they could find for food. Before people learned to farm, they hunted, fished, and gathered food. What they ate depended on where they lived. Today we call this way of life "living off the land."

For about two million years, all people lived off the land. In this article you will read about three groups of people who still live off the land.

Using skills and strategies

Main idea and details

The main idea of a paragraph is what it is mostly about. Details support the main idea by telling more about the main idea. In the first paragraph, the main idea is underlined. The next four sentences are details that tell more about the main idea. Find these sentences. Write *1*, *2*, *3*, and *4* above them.

Australian Aborigines

When you see the word *Aborigine* with a capital *A*, the word means a special group of people. Aborigines are the first people to live on the continent of Australia. The dark part of the map on page 70 that is farthest south shows Australia. Label *Australia* to help you remember where it is.

Aborigines like the ones here were the first people to live in Australia.

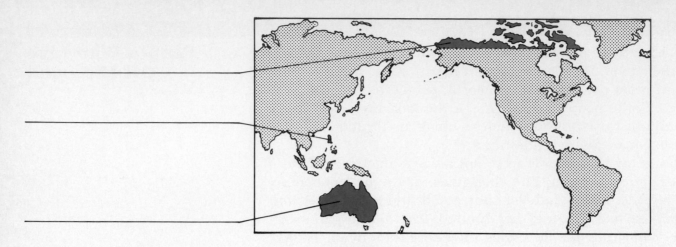

The first Aborigines lived in Australia 40,000 years ago. Today, most Aborigines live in towns and have a modern way of life. Some, however, live as their ancestors did thousands of years ago.

The Aborigines worked hard to get food. They hunted animals and gathered plants to eat. The women caught shellfish, small animals, and insects. They gathered plants that grew in Australia, such as wild yams and water lilies. When a woman gathered the root of a plant, such as a wild yam, she put part of it back in the ground. She did this so the plant would grow back. The women also gathered the seeds of grasses that grew in the desert of Australia.

Using skills and strategies

Main idea and details

A main idea may be stated right in the paragraph. Or the main idea may not be stated, but you can figure it out. Reread the paragraph you just read. The main idea is not stated. Which sentence below states the main idea? Circle it. Then find three details in the paragraph that support your choice. Write *1*, *2*, and *3* next to them.
- Aborigine men and women worked together to gather plants.
- Aborigine women got the food for everyone.

Aborigine men did most of the hunting. They hunted animals and killed them with spears made from stone. Often a group of hunters worked together to catch a large animal. They used spears and nets to catch fish. They also caught turtles, seals, and whales that washed up on the beaches.

Eskimos

Eskimos are people who live in and near the Arctic near the North Pole. Find and label the Arctic on the map.

For thousands of years, Eskimos lived in this cold place. They ate what they could find—mostly animals that lived in the icy lands at the top of the world. They lived on whale, seal, and caribou meat. They usually ate the meat raw because they did not have wood for fires.

Ice fishing is a way the Eskimos of the Arctic caught food thousands of years ago. Today, some of their ancestors fish to make money.

Today, most Eskimos have changed their way of life. Many of them live in towns or villages as you do. But some Eskimos still hunt and fish for most of their food the way their ancestors did. Many Eskimos fish to make money.

Using skills and strategies

Main idea and details

Remember that the main idea of a paragraph tells what the paragraph is mostly about. Reread the paragraphs under the head "Eskimos." Underline the sentence that tells the main idea in each paragraph. You should have underlined three sentences when you are done.

The Tasaday

The Tasaday are about twenty-five people living in a rain forest in the Philippines. Find and label the Philippines on the map.

The Tasaday believe the Owner of All Things made the forest for them to live in and take care of. When they look for food, the Tasaday ask the spirits of the forest if they can gather food there.

Until 1966, the Tasaday lived as Stone Age people. They made tools from stones and pieces of wood. They ate only what they could catch or pick from plants. They did not have metal for traps or tools. The people found tadpoles, frogs, small fish, and crabs in their stream. On land, they gathered yams, fruits, nuts, and bananas.

To the Tasaday, the forest was their whole world. They didn't know there were towns or countries. They knew of only two other groups of people in the forest. Although the

Tasaday didn't see them often, they thought of these people as friends.

In 1966, a man from a tribe the Tasaday did not know came to see them. His name was Dafal. His speech was close enough to theirs so that they could understand each other. Dafal taught the Tasaday how to use traps to catch animals. When the Tasaday ate the meat, they liked it. They thought this was a sign that the Owner of All Things wanted them to eat meat. Dafal gave them knives and showed them how to cut down palm trees to get the starchy food inside them.

One day Dafal invited the Tasaday to go to the edge of the forest to meet someone else. When the Tasaday saw the open land beyond the forest for the first time, they named it the Place Where the Eye Sees Too Far. There they met a person who worked for the government. He was looking for people who might live in the rain forest. Since some people were cutting trees in the rain forest, the government wanted to find the Tasaday and protect them.

The government set aside 46,000 acres of land for the Tasaday. There the Tasaday live much as their ancestors did thousands of years ago.

Think About What You've Read

Important ideas
1. Where does each group described in the article live?

_____

_____

2. What are some foods the Aborigines ate?

_____

_____

3. Why do Eskimos eat plants only at certain times?

_____

_____

Use what you've learned before
4. What do you think American Indians ate a long time ago?

_____

_____

Important word meanings

For each word below, circle a sentence in the article that uses the word. Then write a sentence of your own using each word.

aborigine   **ancestor**   **caribou**

_____

_____

_____

_____

Using skills and strategies

The main idea of an article is what it is mostly about. Write a sentence or two that tells what this article is mostly about.

_____

_____

_____

Writing

Interview an older person. Ask the person about the food he or she ate as a child. How did the person's family get food? In what ways was food different at that time than it is today? After your interview, write a paragraph telling what you learned. Use another sheet of paper for your writing.

Your important ideas

Look back over the article. Write down one idea that seems to be the most important one to you—the one idea that you would like to remember.

_____

_____

Your important words

Look back at the words you have learned as you read about living off the land. Write down the word or words that you think are most important that you would like to remember.

_____

_____

What Happens to the Food You Eat?

What do you already know?

Write down three facts that you already know about what happens to food you eat. If you like, work with a partner.

1. _____

2. _____

3. _____

Make predictions

Look at the pictures, especially the drawing on page 76. Read the headings. Skim the article by reading the first lines of the paragraphs. Then write down two facts that you think you will learn as you read the article.

1. _____

2. _____

Set your purpose for reading

Write down one thing you hope to find out about how your body uses food energy as you read this article.

_____

_____

Learn important words

Study the meanings of the words below and how they are used in sentences. Knowing these words might help you as you read this article.

cell—the basic unit of living matter of which all plants and animals are made. *A cell needs many different nutrients to grow and be healthy.*

energy—the power to work or act. *Your cells burn food to make the energy your body needs to work and grow.*

digest—to change or break down food in the mouth, stomach, and intestines into a form the body can use. *The teeth help digest food by breaking it up into pieces.*

Eating is one of the most important things you do each day. When you eat, you give the cells in your body what they need to grow and do their jobs. One important job of the cells is to make energy. You use this energy for working, playing, and even sleeping. You need energy for everything your body does.

Do you like the food you see in the picture? Do you think the food in the picture is good for you? Yes, pizza is good for you. Pizza has nutrients that help your cells grow and do their jobs. But your cells cannot use the pizza as you see it in the picture. Your body digests, or breaks down, food first. Then food is in a form that your cells can use.

Skills and Strategies

Using a dictionary

A dictionary is a reference you can use to help you find the meanings of words. The next few paragraphs tell how your body digests food. Some words may be new to you. Circle the new words. Before you reread the article, look up the words in a dictionary. Write a meaning for each of the new words in the margin.

How the body digests food

You start to digest food in your mouth. Your teeth cut and tear up food into small pieces. A liquid called saliva in your mouth wets the food. Have you ever tried to swallow a dry piece of bread? Then you know that wet things are easier to swallow than dry ones.

Chewed food leaves your mouth and goes into a long tube called the esophagus. Muscles inside this long tube help push chewed food down and into your stomach.

Skills and strategies

Using a dictionary

The paragraphs on this page tell about the drawing on page 76. On the drawing some of the parts of the body are labeled. If you want more information about these parts, you can look them up in a dictionary. Circle the parts you would like to know more about. Then, before you reread this part of the article, look them up in a dictionary. What can you learn?

Your stomach looks like a large sausage at the bottom of the esophagus. The food you swallow makes the walls of the stomach stretch out. The walls move back and forth to mix and mash the food. Gastric juices pour out of the walls to help break food down. A meal stays in your stomach three or four hours. By then it looks like thick soup.

The Digestive System

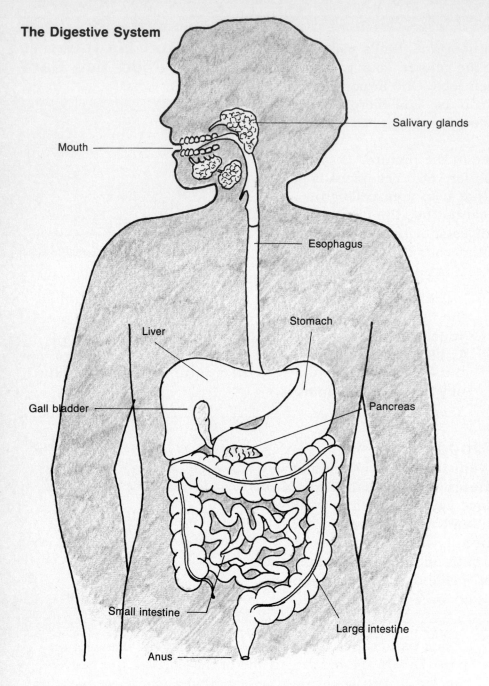

Salivary glands

Mouth

Esophagus

Stomach

Liver

Gall bladder

Pancreas

Small intestine

Large intestine

Anus

Most people think that food is digested in the stomach. That is only partly true. Food is completely digested in the small intestine. The small intestine is really one long tube that is curled up on itself. Liquids from the liver, the pancreas, and the small intestine break food down.

When food leaves the small intestine, it is no longer food as you know it. It is nutrient soup—full of what your cells need to grow and be healthy. Blood picks up these nutrients from the small intestine and carries them to all your body cells.

You eat some foods that your body cannot digest. These foods are only partly broken down. Foods that your body cannot digest are sent into the large intestine. You get rid of this waste material during a bowel movement.

What foods do you need?

All foods provide nutrients your body needs. Some foods provide more of some nutrients than others. Read the chart to learn about nutrients your body needs.

Nutrient	Why You Need It	What Foods Provide It
Carbohydrates	Provide energy	Sugars (milk, dried fruit, honey, beets) and starches (breads, noodles, potatoes)
Fats	Provide energy	Oils, milk, nuts, cheese
Protein	Helps you grow	Meat, poultry, fish, cheese, eggs, dried beans, peanut butter
Vitamins and Minerals	Help your body parts work	A wide variety of fruits and vegetables, including yellow fruits and leafy vegetables; meats, including liver; fish; eggs; whole-grain breads
Water	Needed by every cell	Water, milk, fruits, juices, tomatoes, lettuce

Think About What You've Read

Important ideas

1. What is your body made of?

2. Where does digestion start?

3. Where is most food digested?

4. Why is it healthy to eat many different foods?

Use what you've learned before

5. Which groups of people in Lesson 1 did not have all the nutrients they needed every day? Why?

Important word meanings

Find these words in the lesson: *cell, energy,* and *digest.*
Write the meaning for each one in the margin next to it.
Write your own sentence for each word on the lines below.

_____

_____

_____

_____

Using skills and strategies

Read the words in the list that follows. Circle the words
that name parts of the body. Use a dictionary to help you
find out. You should circle seven words.

liver	blood	nutrient	waste
muscles	stomach	intestine	cell
teeth	gastric	digest	liquid

Writing

On a separate sheet of paper, write a paragraph for a
younger child that tells what happens to food in the
stomach. Make sure that you express the ideas in words a
young child can understand.

Your important ideas

Look back over the article. Write down one idea that
seems to be the most important one to you—the one idea
that you would like to remember.

_____

_____

Your important words

Look back at the words you have learned as you read
about food and digestion. Write down the word or words
that you think are most important—that you would like to
remember.

_____

_____

Jobs People Have in Restaurants

What do you already know?

Write down three facts that you already know about some of the work people do in a restaurant. If you like, work with a partner.

1. _____
2. _____
3. _____

Make predictions

Look at the pictures on pages 80-81. Notice the way the pictures are placed on the pages. Then write down three facts that you think you will learn as you read this article.

1. _____
2. _____
3. _____

Set your purpose for reading

Write down one thing you hope to find out about working in a restaurant as you read this article.

_____

_____

Learn important words

Study the meanings of the words below and how they are used in sentences. Knowing these words might help you as you read this article.

menu—a list of the food served at a meal. *The restaurant menu showed eight different kinds of fish.*

waiter—person who waits on tables and takes orders in a restaurant. *The waiter served lunch.*

busboy—a person who helps the waiter or waitress in a restaurant. *When Joan had the job of busboy, she filled water glasses and took away dirty dishes.*

You can see how food is cooked in many fast-food places. In some, you can even see the packages of bread, boxes of meat patties, and bags of French fries waiting to be cooked. Maybe five or six people work in a fast-food place at a time.

Using skills and strategies

Visualizing

This article has many pictures to help you understand what you read. You know that you won't always have a picture to look at as you read. Many times you have to make the picture in your mind. You use the words you read to visualize. Doing this helps you understand what you read. Reread the first paragraph. What picture do you have in your mind? Is it the same as others in your class?

Many more people work in a large restaurant. Sometimes there will be thirty or forty people who work in a restaurant. When you go to eat in such a place, you will not see the kitchen. You will not see how the food is made or how the dishes are washed. The pictures on these pages show some of the jobs people have in a restaurant.

The meat cook and the baker begin their days early in the morning. The meat cook trims the meat that he will roast later in the day. The baker prepares dough to make hard and soft rolls. Each day, she also bakes a special bread, such as apple or corn bread.

Two customers in the picture below order their meals from the menu. The waiter writes down their choices. The waiter then takes the order to the kitchen where cooks prepare the meals. After the meals are finished, the busboy removes the dirty dishes and takes them to the kitchen to be washed.

Think About What You've Read

Important ideas

1. Why do people who work in a restaurant start work at different times?

_____

_____

_____

2. Who do you think has the most important job in the restaurant? Why?

_____

_____

_____

Use what you've learned before

3. A restaurant usually has many different foods on its menu. Why do you think this is a good idea?

_____

_____

Important Word Meanings

Write two sentences about a restaurant you have been to. Use the words *menu*, *waiter*, and *busboy* in your sentences.

_____

_____

Using skills and strategies

Help someone visualize your favorite food. Write or tell how the food looks, smells, tastes, and feels. Do not say what the food is. See if your friend can guess the food.

Writing

Prepare a breakfast menu for a restaurant called *Better Breakfasts*. Include foods people should eat to get the nutrients they need. Include foods you know people like to eat too. Write your menu on another sheet of paper.

Your important ideas

Look back over the article. Write down one idea that seems to be the most important one to you.

_____

Your important words

Look back at the words you have learned as you read about jobs in restaurants. Write down the word or words that you think are most important.

_____

Questions People Ask About Food

What do you already know?

Write down three questions you have already heard people ask about food and eating. If you like, work with a partner.

1. _____

2. _____

3. _____

Make predictions

Look at the pictures. Read some of the questions that are asked. Then write down three facts that you think you will learn as you read this article.

1. _____

2. _____

3. _____

Set your purpose for reading

Write down one question about food and eating that you hope will be answered as you read this article.

_____

_____

Learn important words

Study the meanings of the words below and how they are used in sentences. Knowing these words might help you as you read this article.

disorder—a sickness or disease. *Sometimes very strong feelings can cause a stomach disorder.*

emotional—having to do with strong feelings. *He had an emotional reaction to the same part of the movie as I did.*

Have you ever written a letter to a newspaper? Students at West High School send their questions about food and eating to the school newspaper. The health teacher writes answers to the questions that are asked the most. Here are some of them.

> Dear Doc,
>   I eat a lot of pizza. Is this bad? Do I have an eating disorder?
>
>   Mac

Mac, didn't you listen in health class when we talked about the basic four food groups? Cheese pizza has foods from three of the groups. The crust is from the bread-cereal group. The sauce and the vegetables are from the fruit-vegetable group. The cheese is from the milk group. You can eat something from the meat group at another meal.

And don't worry. You don't have an eating disorder. It's normal as your body grows to want to eat certain foods all the time. This is all right as long as you eat foods from all the four groups.

> Dear Doc,
>   My sister just broke up with her boyfriend. Now all she does is eat. Is there something wrong with my sister?
>
>   Ruby

Using skills and strategies

Problem and solution

As you read, you often learn about a problem someone has and how that person solves the problem. Very often a person has a choice of how to solve a problem. In her letter, Ruby tells about her sister's problem. It's underlined in the letter. Ruby then says what her sister is doing to solve the problem. What is her sister doing? Write your answer in the margin.

The Basic Four Food Groups

Fruit-vegetable group

Bread-cereal group

Meat group

Milk group

Yes, Ruby, your sister has an emotional problem. And the way she is trying to solve it is not healthy. Your sister is using food to make her feel better. We all are sad at times. We need to find ways other than "pigging out" to make us feel better. If we try to cover up unhappy feelings by eating too much or by not eating anything, we will hurt our bodies. Your sister could try to do something besides eating to make her feel better. She could read some exciting books. She could do an active sport. She could try to meet someone else.

Using skills and strategies

Problem and solution

Doc has other solutions for Ruby's sister. Write one here.

_____

_____

_____

> Dear Doc,
> What is bulimia? I heard a famous actress had it.
> Jay

Jay, bulimia is a serious eating disorder. The person eats and then tries to get rid of the food. The person might vomit or take medicines to empty the intestines. This is how a person gets rid of food so they won't become fat. It sounds strange, but it is really very serious. Bulimia is a serious emotional problem. A person who has this disorder needs help from a doctor.

> Dear Doc,
> I was looking through some old tapes and I came across one by Karen Carpenter. Didn't she starve herself to death? Why would someone do this?
> Jane

You're right, Jane. Karen Carpenter had a serious emotional disorder called anorexia nervosa. Many people—mostly women and young girls—who have this disorder don't like themselves very much. Some doctors think that these people are afraid to face the changes that take place in their bodies and their lives as they grow up. They take out their bad feelings on their bodies and stop eating. They starve themselves to death.

One way people stay healthy is by exercising. Playing tennis is fun and burns up calories.

Dear Doc,
   A girl I see at lunch brags about how much she eats. It's really gross. What really bothers me is that she isn't fat. She has a nice body. How can this be?
   Kurt

Your friend probably gets a lot of exercise. That is the only way to balance the amount of food a person eats. It's a fact. If you eat more food than your body uses, you will store the extra food as fat. If you use all the food you eat, your weight will stay the same. She may talk too much, but she's probably pretty healthy.

Think About What You've Read

Important ideas

1. How can feeling sad make a person want to eat too much?

2. How can exercise help keep a person from becoming overweight?

3. What can happen to a person who has anorexia nervosa?

Use what you've learned before

4. How could the parts of your body be harmed by eating too little food?

_____

_____

_____

Important word meanings

Find and circle the words *disorder* and *emotional* each time they are used in the article. On the lines below, use each word in a sentence about one of the letters you read in the article.

_____

_____

Using skills and strategies

Jay wonders about the problem of bulimia. How does Doc say the problem could be solved? Reread the letter. Then write the solution that Doc suggests.

_____

_____

Writing

You know that people often use food to celebrate happy times. On a sheet of paper, write how your family celebrates a happy event. If food is part of the way you celebrate, write about food. Share your paragraphs with others in your class if you would like to.

Your important ideas

Look back over the article. Write down one idea that seems to be the most important one to you—the one idea that you would like to remember.

_____

_____

Your important words

Look back at the words you have learned as you read the questions and answers about food. Write down the word or words that you think are most important—that you would like to remember.

_____

_____

Reviewing What You Have Learned

Some facts and ideas you have learned

You learned many important facts and ideas as you read about food. A few of them are listed below. Add your own important ideas to the end of this list. You can look back at the "Your important ideas" section of each lesson to remember the ideas you wrote down.

- Thousands of years ago, people got their food by hunting, fishing, and gathering wild plants.
- You start to digest food you eat in your mouth when you chew.
- In a restaurant, a food preparation worker gets salads, desserts, and sandwiches ready to serve.
- Sometimes people use food to make themselves feel better or to show they are unhappy about their lives.

_____

_____

_____

Some word meanings you have learned

Here are some of the important words you learned in the articles you read. Make sure you understand their meanings. Then add important words of your own. You can look back at the "Your important words" section of each lesson to remember the words you wrote down.

ancestor—a person who lived a long time ago in a family. _Tina's ancestors handed down special recipes for holidays._

digest—to change or break down food in the mouth, stomach, and intestines into a form the body can use. _The walls of the stomach help to digest food._

menu—a list of the food served at a meal. _Each student gets a copy of the school menu at the beginning of the month._

_____

_____

_____

Purposes for reading

Look back at the section at the beginning of every lesson called "Set your purpose for reading." Write down one of the purposes you set for reading that you want to remember. Did you meet this purpose? If not, how can you meet it?

_____

_____

Using skills and strategies

If you like, work with a partner. Think up one or two problems people your age have concerning food or eating. Write down the problems on the lines below. Then trade papers with another pair of students. Read the problems. Together, write a solution for each problem.

_____

_____

_____

_____

_____

Writing: opinion

Imagine that you lived long ago in one of the groups you read about in "People Who Live Off the Land." On a sheet of paper, write a paragraph telling which group you would prefer to live in and why. Use examples from the article to explain your reasons.

Revising

Go back and read what you wrote about living off the land. Check these things:

1. Would someone reading your paragraph understand why you chose the group you did?
2. Do you have a main idea and details supporting the main idea? Change your paragraph, if necessary, to include a main idea and details.

Activities

1. Choose a food-related topic to learn more about. Some examples are: world hunger, sports nutrition, food in other countries, or calories in food. Go to the library and find one or two books or magazine articles about your topic. Tell the class what you learned.
2. Read all or part of _Food for Today's Teens: Common Sense Nutrition for Fun and Fitness_ by Fredrick Stare and Virginia Aronson (Stickley, 1985). Make a list of five ideas you think are important to remember.
3. Invent a Basic Four Sandwich and a Basic Four Drink. For each, put together foods from each of the Basic Four Food Groups. Can you do it?
4. Write an ad for your favorite food. Use music, art, poetry, or any other way you can think of to tell others why your food is great.

Law

Read and learn about law

The picture on the next page shows the United States Capitol Building in Washington, D.C. The people who work there are legislators. They make up the U.S. Congress that votes to make our national laws. One of the President's jobs is to make sure citizens follow the laws passed by Congress. The judges of the Supreme Court decide if the laws are in keeping with the Constitution of the United States.

What do you already know about law?

Talk about what you know. Get together with a group of students to talk about what you already know about law. Here are some questions to get you started.

1. Is making laws new to people? Or have people always had laws?
2. How are your state laws made?
3. Have there ever been bad laws?

Write about what you know. Think of two laws you know. Write them down. Tell why each law is important.

_____

_____

_____

_____

_____

Make predictions

Read the titles of the articles in this cluster and look at the picture on page 91. Write down three things you think you'll learn by reading these articles about law.

1. _____

2. _____

3. _____

Start to learn new word meanings

All the words listed below are used in the paragraph at the top of page 90. Study the meanings of these words as you read about law.

legislator—a person who makes laws. *The legislator studied the law about the rights of children.*

citizen—a person who is a member of a nation. *An adult citizen has the right to vote.*

constitution—a document that tells how a country, state, or group will be run. *The state constitution tells how long the governor will be in office.*

Learn new skills and strategies

Some information you read is easier to understand if it is arranged briefly in a table. For example, a table of contents lets you locate the page number of any selection in a book quickly. In this cluster, one of the skills you will learn is how to use tables to find information quickly and easily.

Gather new information

By the end of this cluster, you will have learned the answers to these questions.

1. What system of laws is the U.S. system based on?
2. What does a legislator do?
3. What are some laws that affect teenagers?
4. What rights did slaves have in our country in the 1800s?

Why People Need Laws

What do you already know?
Write down three facts you already know about why people need laws. Work with a partner, if you like.

1. _____

2. _____

3. _____

Make predictions
Look at the pictures and the headings in large type in the article. Then write down three facts you think you will learn as you read this article.

1. _____

2. _____

3. _____

Set your purpose for reading
Write down one thing you hope to find out about why people need laws as you read this article.

_____

_____

Learn important words
Study the meanings of the words below and how they are used in sentences. Knowing these words might help you as you read this article.

constitution—a document that tells how a country, state, or group will be run. *The people voted for a new state constitution.*

law—a rule that must be obeyed. *There is a law against young children working in our country.*

right—fair treatment; something that is due to a person. *Our right to go to church is protected by law.*

legal—lawful or according to the law. *The sale of fireworks is legal in some states but not in others.*

At the beginning of each school year, students and teachers usually talk about school rules. Some rules explain how the students will act toward each other. Some tell how teachers and other adults will treat the students. The teachers also explain what will happen if the students break rules. In some schools, students and teachers work together to decide many of the rules they follow in school. These rules may be put together in a school constitution.

When people work together writing rules for themselves, they follow a very old tradition. For as long as men and women have lived on Earth, they have lived in groups. Some of these groups are: families, tribes, towns, cities, states, and nations. Each group needs rules to explain the duties and rights of its members. Groups also need rules to explain what members cannot do. We call these rules laws.

Using skills and strategies
Clarifying

You often hear words or ideas that aren't clear to you. When you pick out these words and ideas and try to find out what they mean, you are *clarifying*.

Look back over the first two paragraphs. Circle any words you don't know and write them in the margin. Before you continue reading, find out what the words mean by talking with another student. Asking someone else is one way to clarify meanings. Write the words' meanings in the margin.

All groups of people have laws and rules, including students in a classroom. In some schools, both students and teachers decide the rules they will obey.

Laws telling people how to act go back thousands of years. The King of Babylon, Hammurabi, wrote his laws on thumb-shaped tablets.

Laws of ancient people

We do not know exactly what rules the first people lived by. This is because they did not have a way to write down their rules. Writing developed about six thousand years ago. Then people could write down their rules. The oldest written laws were made in the Middle East 3,700 years ago. These laws said that people could not steal, do poor work, or hit another person.

Some people think of a man named Moses when they think of the laws of ancient people. Moses was a leader and a teacher of the Hebrew people about 3,200 years ago. A story in the Bible tells how God gave Moses a set of laws called the Ten Commandments. These laws told the people how to act. For example, they could not steal, lie, or murder. They had to show respect for each other. The Ten Commandments were needed because Moses's people had to work together to survive in the desert.

Using skills and strategies

Clarifying

Are you finding more words you don't know? Sometimes hard words name people and places. Circle these words as you go along. You can often clarify the meanings of names and places by looking them up in a dictionary. Look up *Moses* in a dictionary. In the margin, write down what you find.

Keep circling words you don't know.

The beginnings of law in the United States

You know that people from other countries settled in America. Many of these people came from England. They brought their laws and the English way of making laws with them.

The laws in England were known as common laws. People all over England accepted these laws. If people broke these laws, they were punished. Common laws protected people's rights. Our legal system began with English common laws.

The English people who came to America thought each person had rights that should be protected. For example, they believed they should be free to practice their religion. They felt that people should be able to decide about the taxes they should pay. When the king of England tried to take their rights away, the colonists went to war with England. That war was the Revolutionary War.

The signing of the Constitution took courage from a number of brave people who wanted freedom.

During the Revolutionary War, the Americans started their own government. They felt strongly that there should be laws to protect the rights of every person. When the Americans won the war, they wrote down these laws in the United States Constitution. The Constitution was written over two hundred years ago. However, it still protects the rights of every person in the United States.

Using skills and strategies

Clarifying

Before you finish the article, look back at the words you have circled. Have you been able to clarify their meanings? If not, talk to someone else about them, or look them up in a dictionary. Then write what the words mean in the margins.

Our Laws Today

Today there are laws that cover many activities of our lives. The Congress passes laws about things covered in the U.S. Constitution. States pass laws about things that are not covered in the Constitution. These laws help Americans work and live together. They protect people and property from harm. Laws help prevent confusion in business. Laws tell how people should be punished if they do not follow the laws.

Think About What You've Read

Important Ideas
1. Why don't we know what laws the first people had?

_____

_____

2. Name some early laws. Why do you think people had laws about these things?

_____

_____

_____

Use what you've learned before
3. What are three ways laws are important for people in the United States today?

_____

_____

_____

Important word meanings

On a sheet of paper, make a crossword puzzle. Use the words *legislator*, *law*, *citizen*, and *legal*. First attach the words to each other for the puzzle.

When all the words are in your puzzle, get a clean sheet of paper and draw boxes to take the place of the letters. Number each box that will begin a word.

Write the headings *Across* and *Down* and make up a meaning clue for each word. Number your clues to match the numbers in the boxes. Give your puzzle to a friend to do.

Using skills and strategies

As you read this article, you tried to clarify words and names that you did not know. List the words and write a sentence for each one. Include these words too: *legal*, *constitution*, *law*, and *right*.

_____

_____

_____

_____

_____

Writing

Suppose you and a group of people your age are stranded on an island. After a while, some people begin doing things that are unfair to others. You decide the group needs a set of laws. On a separate sheet of paper, write down some laws you think your group should have. Be ready to share your ideas with others.

Your important ideas

Look back over the article. Write down one idea that seems to be the most important one to you—the one idea that you would like to remember.

_____

_____

Your important words

Look back at the words you have learned as you read about why people need laws. Write down the word or words you would most like to remember.

_____

_____

Students as Lawmakers

What do you already know?

Write down three facts you already know about how state laws are made. Work with a partner, if you like.

1. _____

2. _____

3. _____

Make predictions

Look at the photographs and the table in the article. Then write down three facts you think you will learn as you read this article.

1. _____

2. _____

3. _____

Set your purpose for reading

Write down one thing you hope to find out about students as lawmakers as you read this article.

_____

_____

Learn important words

Study the meanings of the words below and how they are used in sentences. Knowing these words might help you as you read this article.

legislator—a person who makes laws. *The legislators passed a law about car safety.*

lobby—try to influence legislators or other public officials. *The teachers plan to lobby to get more money for schools.*

bill—a law presented to legislators. *A legislator wrote a bill that banned smoking in public.*

majority—the largest part of a group. *A bill must get a majority of votes to become a law.*

By 5:15 A.M., Andrea was packed and ready to go. She met a few of her classmates and teachers at Near North High School in Chicago, Illinois. Their bus left for Springfield, Illinois at 6:00 A.M. They would take part in the Illinois YMCA Youth and Government Conference.

High school students from all over Illinois acted out the jobs of people in government for three days. They elected a governor and other state officers. They lobbied and passed laws. They argued cases in front of a student court. The table shows some of the roles the students took.

Using skills and strategies

Using Pictorial Aids: Tables

A table gives you a lot of information without too many words. A table has a title and headings that name the information in each column. The table that follows gives the names of different jobs people have in state governments. It tells what the person in each job does. Andrea was a legislator. Circle the information on the table that tells about her job.

Jobs in Government	
Name of Job	**What the Person Does**
Governor	Directs the state government, enforces the laws, and suggests bills
Lieutenant Governor	Helps the governor and takes over if the governor dies
President of the Senate	Runs the meetings of the Senate
Speaker of the House	Runs the meetings of the House of Representatives
Legislator	Suggests bills and votes on bills as a member of either the House of Representatives or the Senate
Clerk	Records what happens at the meetings of the House or the Senate
Page	Takes messages between the House and Senate
Sergeant-at-Arms	Maintains order in House and Senate
Judge	Hears and decides cases in court
Bailiff	Takes charge of members of the jury and guards prisoners while in court

Andrea and her classmates load the bus for Springfield.

A student gives a speech asking people to elect her governor.

A student legislator argues for the bill he wants passed.

A newspaper reporter types out a story about the day's activities.

Some students at the Youth and Government Conference work as reporters in a TV studio.

A young lobbyist asks the legislators to defeat a bill she opposes.

Andrea went to Springfield because her school's class wrote a bill that other students thought should be a law. The bill would ban smoking in places where people work.

In Springfield, Andrea acted as a legislator. She met with other legislators to discuss her bill and their bills. During the meetings, Andrea listened to lobbyists. They told her why they thought certain bills should be passed. Andrea took part in discussions about her bill. She talked about other bills that had to do with selling fireworks and making it safer for people who worked in coal mines. Andrea tried to decide which of their bills she would vote for. She wondered whether the other legislators would vote for her bill.

After the meetings were over, Andrea worked on her bill some more. She changed it in certain ways to satisfy the other legislators.

Andrea told a newspaper reporter about the changes she had made in her bill. The reporter wrote about the changes in that day's newspaper. That night, Andrea appeared on the TV news along with the student governor. The governor said she thought Andrea's bill was good. She said she would sign it if it passed the House and the Senate.

Using Skills and Strategies

Using Pictorial Aids: Tables

Do you know what the governor of a state does? Find the job, governor, on the table on page 99. Underline what the governor does.

On Sunday, Andrea presented her bill to the legislature. She thought a majority of the legislators would vote for it. When the votes were counted, her bill had passed both the House and the Senate. Then it went to the governor's office. The student governor signed the bill into law.

What Andrea and the other students did that weekend was important. First, they learned how a bill becomes a law. Then they learned that a bill doesn't become a law just because one person thinks it should. Many people have to believe it should be a law. Before a bill becomes law, many people talk about it. It is changed and changed again. Only when it satisfies the majority of legislators will it become a law.

Working together to make laws that are fair is one way legislators help protect people's rights. Andrea and the other students learned this important idea firsthand in Springfield.

Think About What You've Read

Important ideas
1. Who is in charge of the meetings of the Senate of Illinois?

_____

2. What people are involved in making a bill a state law?

_____

_____

3. Who decides whether a bill becomes a law?

_____

_____

Use what you've learned before
4. What laws can state legislators make?

_____

_____

Important word meanings

The words *lobby, bill, majority, law, legislator,* and *right* have to do with the way people work to make a bill into a law. Write two or three sentences about how a bill becomes a law. Use at least four of the vocabulary words.

_____

_____

_____

Using skills and strategies

Look back at the table on page 99. Then complete a table of your own. Use the title and the headings below. Fill in at least three jobs. Add more, if you wish.

Jobs in a School	
Name of Job	What the Person Does

Writing

This article tells about some of the jobs a person might have in state government. By taking part in the conference, Andrea found out what it would be like to be a legislator. On a separate sheet of paper, write a paragraph about how a legislator might spend his or her day.

Your important ideas

Look back over the article. Write down one idea that seems to be the most important one to you—the one idea that you would like to remember.

_____

_____

Your important words

Look back at the words you have learned as you read "Students as Lawmakers." Write down the word or words that you think are most important—that you would like to remember.

_____

_____

Laws You Should Know

What do you already know?
Write down three facts that you already know about laws that affect you. Work with a partner, if you like.

1. _____

2. _____

3. _____

Make predictions
Look at the pictures, the table, and the headings in the article. Then write down three facts you think you will learn as you read this article.

1. _____

2. _____

3. _____

Set your purpose for reading
Write down one thing you hope to find out about laws you should know as you read this article.

_____

_____

Learn important words
Study the meanings of the words below and how they are used in sentences. Knowing these words might help you read this article.

minor—a person under the age of responsibility. *The law decides when a minor becomes an adult.*

citizen—a person who is a member of a nation. *A person must be an American citizen to vote in a presidential election.*

civil rights—human rights a government gives citizens. *American blacks fought a long battle to gain full civil rights.*

Legislators in the Congress pass new laws each year. In addition, each state passes more laws. There are so many laws that it would take years to read them all. You will probably never need to know all of the laws. But there are some you should know about.

In the United States, laws fall into two broad groups: private law and public law. Private law sets rules for the ways people deal with each other. Public law sets rules for the ways people deal with society as a whole.

Private and Public Law	
Private Law Sets Rules About:	**Public Law Sets Rules About:**
Renting an apartment	Civil rights
Buying a home	Printing money
Getting married	Crimes such as stealing and damage to property
Getting divorced	Crimes such as murder and kidnapping
Personal injuries, as in a traffic accident	Taxes
Writing a will	Protecting the environment
Starting a business	Protecting people who buy products

Sometimes people think of laws in terms of crime and punishment. For example, if a young man steals something, he will be punished. If he is a minor, he probably won't go to jail. He may do service work or go to a counselor instead.

Laws do more than set punishments. Laws protect your rights as a citizen. Read the following stories to learn about some private laws and some public laws that might affect you and other young people.

Using skills and strategies

Drawing conclusions

A conclusion is a decision you reach after thinking about some facts and details. Each story that follows gives you some facts and then comes to a conclusion. Underline the conclusion in each story. The first one is done for you.

Can a principal search a student's locker?

Janis is known as someone who sells illegal pills in school. Of course, this is against school rules. It is also against a state law. On hearing a rumor that Janis sells pills, the principal searches her locker. He finds some pills. He calls the police. They arrest Janis.

Janis must go to court. She broke a state law by having the pills. But she says the principal violated her civil rights by searching her locker without her permission. What do you think?

The court sided with the principal—even though Janis is partly right. The Constitution protects people from unreasonable searches. However, the court says that the principal's search was reasonable because he had some evidence that she was breaking the law. (He had heard rumors.) If there had been no evidence, the principal would not have had the right to search Janis's locker.

Is a parent responsible for a child's actions?

Let's assume you are a lot older and that you have a son. You live in an area that is not very crowded and your son wants an air rifle. You give it to him, and together you set down the rules for using it. Your son doesn't follow the rules as he promised. He shoots at birds, at small animals, and at windows. The neighbors complain to you. You talk to your son, but he doesn't listen. Finally, a shot from the gun hurts a child. The child's parents take you to court, asking for a large amount of money. Will you have to pay?

Yes, you will. You must take responsibility because your son acted badly many times. He used the rifle in a dangerous way. The history of poor behavior makes your son's actions your responsibility.

Can you return something bought on sale?

You buy a sweater during a sale. At home you discover that the sweater has a big hole in it. You go back to the store, but the clerk tells you that all sales are final, and that you have to live with your purchase. Do you?

ALL SALES FINAL!

No, you don't. People do not have to keep things they buy that don't work or are broken or torn. In general, things you buy must meet certain standards. The sweater does not meet the standards. You have every right to demand and get your money back.

Can parents take a minor's paycheck?

José is excited about his first paycheck. He feels he really worked hard and deserves to spend a little of it. He asks his girlfriend to go to the movies. However, his mother insists that José give her his paycheck. José's mother gives him the money he needs for the date. But José isn't happy about losing the rest of his paycheck. Is it legal for his mother to take his paycheck?

Yes. José's parents can take his paycheck. This is because José lives at home and is a minor. As a minor, José doesn't have the same civil rights that an adult would have.

Think About What You've Read

Important ideas
1. List two activities that fall under private law.

_____

_____

2. List two activities that fall under public law.

_____

_____

3. Is the law fair when it allows a principal to search a student's locker? Give reasons for your answer.

_____

_____

_____

Use what you've learned before
4. What person in government has the job of hearing and deciding on cases such as Janis's?

_____

_____

Important word meanings

On the lines below, write sentences using the words *minor, citizen, majority,* and *legal.*

_____

_____

_____

_____

Write a sentence using the term *civil rights.*

_____

Using skills and strategies

Look back at each story you read. Find the conclusion you underlined in each story. Circle the facts and details that led to the conclusions. You should circle one or two facts for each story. Write two facts about one of the stories on the lines below.

_____

_____

Writing

On a separate sheet of paper, list four things you do often. Next to each one, write whether or not a law controls the activity. For example, if you ride a bus, there are traffic laws involved. If you buy a carton of milk, there are health and safety laws involved.

Your important ideas

Look back over the article. Write down one idea that seems to be the most important one to you—the one idea that you would like to remember.

_____

_____

Your important words

Look back at the words you have learned as you read about laws you should know. Write down the word or words that you think are most important—that you would like to remember.

_____

_____

The Law That Helped Start a War

What do you already know?

Write down three facts you already know about the Civil War. Work with a partner, if you like.

1. _____
2. _____
3. _____

Make predictions

Look at the pictures and the headings in the article. Then write down three facts you think you will learn as you read this article.

1. _____
2. _____
3. _____

Set your purpose for reading

Write down what you hope to find out about the law that helped start a war as you read this article.

_____

_____

Learn important words

Study the meanings of the words below and how they are used in sentences. Knowing these words might help you as you read this article.

slavery—the custom of owning slaves. *Many people opposed slavery because it allowed people to be bought and sold.*

plantation—a large farm where crops such as cotton, tobacco, and sugar cane are grown. *The plantations of the South grew cotton and tobacco.*

economy—the way goods and services are made, bought, and sold. *Slaves made the economy of the South work.*

The U.S. Constitution says that all citizens are free and equal. However, in the past, not everybody was free and equal.

Using skills and strategies

Clarifying

When you read an article about history, there will be ideas as well as words you need to clarify. As you read, underline ideas that you don't understand. Then watch and see if the rest of the article explains them. Write ideas you want to clarify in the margins.

The South and slavery

Between 1810 and 1860, cotton was king in the South. More and more people moved into the southern states of Alabama, Mississippi, Arkansas, and Texas. They turned huge areas of land into plantations and grew cotton. Cotton became the South's main crop.

The cotton plantations were so large that the owners could not do the work. Black slaves did the work. Slaves were not free people. They were the property of the plantation owners. Slaves had few civil rights. They could not move freely from place to place and they couldn't own land. As property, slaves were bought, sold, and traded by their owners.

Slaves planted and picked cotton on southern plantations in the mid 1800s. Cotton was the South's main crop and was very important to the economy.

Harriet Tubman, far left, led many slaves to freedom on the Underground Railroad. The Underground Railroad was a route of safe hiding places that helped southern slaves escape to free states in the North.

Using skills and strategies

Clarifying

Suppose you wanted to clarify the phrase, "slaves were bought, sold, and traded by their owners." You could look in an encyclopedia under *Slavery* and learn more. Continue to write ideas that need clarifying in the margins.

Most people who lived in the North did not own slaves. People in the northern states of Illinois, Michigan, Wisconsin, and Iowa had small farms. Families, not slaves, worked the farms.

People in the New England states did not own slaves either. Many of them worked in factories that made things. Farmers in New England worked their own farms too. Thus, the northern economy did not depend on slaves to make it work.

How people felt about slavery

Different people had different ideas about slavery. Southerners depended on slaves to plant, pick, and pack their cotton. Their economy was based on slavery. And, in all southern states, owning slaves was legal.

Northerners didn't need slaves to help their economy. Many northerners felt it was wrong to treat people as property. In the North, it was against the law to own slaves. Many people there wanted to end slavery in the United States.

Because northern states didn't allow slavery, slaves wanted to go there to live. Getting to a free state was very hard. Many northerners helped slaves go north by providing places they could hide. This route they followed to the North was called the Underground Railroad. People who

Dred Scott

were part of the Underground Railroad helped slaves get across slave states and into free states. Many slaves made it to freedom in this way, but many did not. Some were caught and returned to their owners. Often they were punished for running away.

A slave goes to court

Some slaves tried to gain their freedom by going to court. There they tried to show that slavery wasn't legal. The most famous case of this kind involved Dred Scott. Dred Scott belonged to a doctor in the U.S. Army named John Emerson. In 1835, Emerson took Scott from Missouri (a slave state) to Wisconsin (a free state). A few years later John Emerson died. Dred Scott then became the property of Emerson's wife. She took him back to Missouri.

Dred Scott sued Emerson's wife for his freedom. That is, he took her to court. He wanted the court to make him a free man. He believed that, since he had lived in a free state, he should be free. However, the Missouri Supreme Court ruled against him.

But the case was not over. During the trial, Emerson's wife sold Dred Scott to a man named John Sanford. Dred Scott took his case to a U.S. Court. Would the U.S. Court free Dred Scott? No, the U.S. Court ruled against him, too. Finally, the United States Supreme Court agreed to hear Dred Scott's case.

The U.S. Supreme Court and Dred Scott

That the U.S. Supreme court took the case shows how important it had become. The Supreme Court chooses the cases it hears. And, what it decides becomes the law of the land.

By 1850, the United States was almost two countries—the North and the South. The South wanted slavery to be legal throughout the nation. The North did not. People in some parts of the United States had begun fighting and killing each other over slavery. Some people felt slavery would break the country apart. They wanted the Supreme Court to decide whether slavery was going to be legal or not in the United States.

When Dred Scott took his case to the Supreme Court, both the North and the South were watching. The judges on the Supreme Court listened carefully to the case. On March 6, 1857, Chief Justice Roger B. Taney read what they had decided. The decision shocked many people.

The Supreme Court ruled against Dred Scott. They said he couldn't have his freedom. In fact, they said he didn't even have the right to take his case to court. They ruled that, as a slave, Dred Scott was not a citizen of the United States. The Court also said that no black person, free or slave, could ever be a citizen of the United States.

The Court said that Congress could not pass laws to ban slavery. This would violate a person's right to own property.

Many people were angry and troubled by what the Supreme Court said. People who felt slavery was bad worked even harder against it. These people believed that every person had a right to be free.

Eventually, the country fought the Civil War over the slavery issue. Hundreds of thousands of people died so that Dred Scott and other black people could be free.

Think About What You've Read

Important ideas

1. In what way did the economy of the South depend on slavery?

_____

_____

2. Why did slaves want to go north to live?

_____

_____

3. Why did Dred Scott feel the court would grant his freedom?

_____

_____

4. What did the Supreme Court decide in the Dred Scott Case?

_____

_____

_____

Use what you've learned before

5. How did slavery affect a slave's civil rights?

_____

_____

Important word meanings

Find the words *slavery*, *plantation*, *civil rights*, *citizen*, and *economy* in the article. Underline a sentence in which each word appears. Write a sentence of your own using the words.

_____

_____

_____

_____

_____

Using skills and strategies

Write down a word or phrase you didn't understand as you read this article. Tell what it means. Tell how you found out what it means.

_____

_____

_____

Writing

Pretend you are a news reporter. You have been sent to cover the Dred Scott story. You plan to talk to Dred Scott about his life as a slave. Write down three questions you will ask him. Do not write any questions he can answer with only *yes* or *no*.

_____

_____

_____

Your important ideas

Look back over the article. Write down one idea that seems to be the most important one to you—the one idea that you would like to remember.

_____

Your important words

Look back at the words you have learned as you read this article. Write down the word or words that you think are most important—that you would like to remember.

_____

_____

Reviewing What You Have Learned

Some facts and ideas you have learned

You learned many important facts and ideas as you read about law. A few of them are listed below. Add your own important ideas to the end of this list. You can look back at the "Your important ideas" section of each lesson to remember the ideas you wrote down.

- The U. S. legal system is based on the English common-law system.
- A state legislator works to pass laws that a majority of legislators believe are good.
- Teenagers are covered by many laws that affect adults. But, as minors, they have fewer civil rights than adults.
- Slaves had almost no rights in this country.

_____

_____

_____

_____

_____

Some word meanings you have learned

Here are some of the important words you learned in the articles you read. Make sure you understand their meanings. Then add important words of your own. You can look back at the "Your important words" section of each lesson to remember the words you wrote down.

legal—lawful or according to the law. *The sale of fireworks is legal in some states but not in others.*

minor—a person under the age of responsibility. *A minor has fewer rights than an adult.*

civil rights—human rights a government gives citizens. *Slaves did not have any civil rights.*

_____

_____

_____

Purposes for reading

Look back at the section at the beginning of every lesson called "Set your purpose for reading." What purposes did you set for reading the articles in this cluster? Tell where you might find information to help you achieve one of your purposes.

_____

_____

Using skills and strategies

The table that follows lists problems and solutions you read about in this cluster. Fill in a missing problem or solution. One is done for you.

How People Solved Problems

Problem	Solution
American colonists thought England was violating their rights.	Colonists fought the Revolutionary War for their freedom.
Early people needed ways to keep people from stealing each other's things.	_____ _____
_____ _____	Andrea made many changes in her bill to satisfy the legislators.
A student buys a sweater that is ripped.	_____ _____
Slavery kept blacks from being free.	_____ _____

Writing: personal opinion

Think about something you feel should be a law. On a sheet of paper, write a paragraph that tells what your law would be. Tell why you think it is important.

Revising

Discuss your law with a classmate. Ask if he or she has any suggestions for changing your law. Then change the law you wrote to include the comments from your classmate.

Activities

1. Read about the judicial system in *The American Legal System* by E. B. Fincher (Watts: 1980). If you find this book at a library, look at the other books on the shelves near it. They will be about the courts too. Check out the ones that interest you.
2. Look through your local newspaper for news stories that refer to laws. Report to the class about the article that interests you the most.
3. Talk to someone who works at a job you'd like to learn more about. Find out what laws affect the work this person does. Tell the class what you learned.

Space

Read and learn about space

Our planet is surrounded by a blanket of air called the atmosphere. People need the gases in the atmosphere to live. Yet for almost thirty years, astronauts have gone beyond our atmosphere. They have traveled into the huge area of space where there is no air and no life. These people—guided by others on the ground—would quickly die without their protective suits.

The astronauts' courage has answered some questions we have about our Earth and its solar system. However, their travels have also raised new questions we have yet to answer.

What do you already know about space?

Talk about what you know. Get together with a group of students to talk about what you already know about space. Here are some questions to help you get started.
1. What things are in space beyond the Earth?
2. Why is space so dangerous to people?
3. Where have people and their spacecraft traveled so far?

Write about what you know. Write a brief paragraph that tells about a real trip people have made into space. Tell whether you think the trip was a good idea or not.

_____

_____

_____

_____

Make predictions

Read the titles of the articles in this cluster and look at the picture on page 121. Write down three things that you think you'll learn by reading these articles about space.

1. _____

2. _____

3. _____

Start to learn new word meanings

All of the words listed below are used in the two paragraphs on page 120. Study the meanings of these words as you read about space.

atmosphere—the layer of gases that surrounds the Earth. *The atmosphere gets thinner as you travel away from the Earth.*

astronaut—a pilot or a member of the crew of a spacecraft. *The astronaut hopped along the surface of the moon.*

solar system—the sun and all the planets and other bodies that move around the sun. *There are nine planets in the solar system.*

Learn new skills and strategies

One of the strategies you will learn about in this cluster is semantic mapping. This strategy helps you explore the connection between new information and the things you already know.

Gather new information

By the end of this cluster, you will have learned the answers to these questions.

1. Where does space start?
2. How did *Skylab* prove that people could live in space?
3. Why do astronauts need to know how to get food in a desert or a jungle?
4. How might a star have caused all the dinosaurs to die?

Journey From Earth Through Space

What do you already know?

Write three facts that you already know about travel through space. Work with a partner, if you like.

1. _____
2. _____
3. _____

Make predictions

Look at the photographs and the diagram. Quickly skim the article. Then write down three facts that you think you will learn as you read this article.

1. _____
2. _____
3. _____

Set your purpose for reading

Write down one thing you hope to find out about space as you read this article.

_____

_____

Learn important words

Study the meanings of the words below and how they are used in sentences. Knowing these words might help you as you read this article.

atmosphere—the layer of gases that surrounds the Earth. *The atmosphere forms a protective blanket around Earth.*

satellite—a body in space that moves around a planet. *Our moon is the Earth's satellite.*

orbit—the path of a body in space around another. *The Earth orbits the sun and the moon orbits the Earth.*

solar system—the sun and the planets and other bodies that move around it. *The sun is the center of the solar system.*

3...2...1...blast-off! You hear the roar of the rockets. You feel the seat move under you. Tons of fuel burn and push you up, up, faster and faster. We're off for a trip through space.

To even get to space, we must first go through the Earth's atmosphere—a thick blanket of air. Space begins about 100 miles above the Earth. In space, there isn't much air. However, there is gravity. Gravity keeps man-made satellites from flying off into space.

Using skills and strategies

Semantic mapping

Semantic mapping is a way to group ideas or words. Keeping words or ideas that are alike together helps you remember what you know. It helps you put new information in helpful places in your mind. For example, *blast-off, rockets,* and *fuel* all have to do with getting to space. What word in the second paragraph above makes you think of space? Circle that word.

We continue to move away from Earth. After 2½ days, we've traveled 240,000 miles. We're only 100 miles from the moon. The moon is Earth's satellite and our nearest neighbor in space. Earth's gravity keeps the moon moving around it.

We touch down on the moon. Solid ground again! It looks a little like Earth, almost safe. But is it like Earth? If you try to talk or sing or whistle, no sound comes out. That's because sound on Earth moves through air, and there's no air here. No air also means you can't breathe here without taking your own air along.

Look around. There's no water on the moon either. In fact, there are no plants, animals, or other forms of life on the moon. Life as we know it needs both air and water to live.

Distances from Earth to Bodies in Space

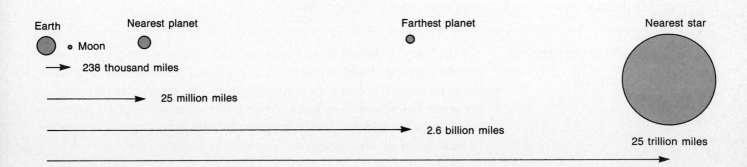

| Earth | Nearest planet | | Farthest planet | | Nearest star |

238 thousand miles

25 million miles

2.6 billion miles

25 trillion miles

Astronauts first landed on the moon in 1969. Because gravity is less on the moon, the astronauts were able to move easily in their heavy spacesuits.

People landed on the moon for the first time in 1969. Astronauts wore special suits and carried their own air to walk on the moon. Their suits protected them from the very high temperatures during the moon day. Half the moon always faces the sun, and the moon has no atmosphere to block any of the sun's rays. Therefore, the temperature on the moon in the middle of the day is about 250°F.

One thing is easier on the moon than on the Earth—walking. It's easier because the moon's gravity is less than the Earth's gravity. This means you feel lighter. Wearing a heavy spacesuit is easy because the moon's pull on you is one-sixth as much as the Earth's pull on you.

When we go away from the moon instead of back to Earth, we go where no one has ever gone before. We enter interplanetary space, or the space between the planets. The Earth is one of nine planets that orbit, or move in a set way, around the sun. The sun and all the planets and other bodies that move around it make up our solar system.

Although people have not gone beyond the moon, we have sent rockets out past the moon and into space. These rockets fly by, orbit, or land on the planets. They send back pictures and information. In this way we learn much about Mars, Venus, Mercury, Jupiter, Saturn, and Uranus.

Getting the pictures and information takes a long time because the distance between the planets is so huge. For example, Pioneer 10 left the Earth in March, 1972. It came within 81,000 miles of Jupiter twenty-one months later. Pioneer 10 didn't leave the solar system until June, 1983.

Using skills and strategies

Semantic mapping

You have learned new facts to add to the ones you already know about space. Think about how the facts could be grouped. Here are two ideas: *facts about the moon* and *facts about space*. Go back over what you have read and find facts to add to these groups. Write *moon* or *space* next to the facts in the margin.

We will go out past the planets on our journey. When we leave interplanetary space, we enter the space between the stars. The distances here are so great they are hard to imagine. To get to the closest star past the sun, we would need to travel 25 trillion miles. Suppose a baby left the Earth in a spaceship traveling at the speed of 66 million miles per hour. That baby would be an old person by the time he or she visits the nearest star and returns home.

Our solar system and the nearest stars are just a small part of a galaxy. Galaxies are groups of stars, dust, and gas. Gravity holds the stars, dust, and gas together.

Scientists believe there are billions of galaxies scattered throughout space. A large galaxy may have a trillion stars. A small one may have only a few billion. Our galaxy is called the Milky Way. On a clear night away from city lights, you can see it as a wide band of stars in the sky. Traveling to the stars seems impossible today. But don't forget that people long ago thought walking on the moon was only a dream.

Think About What You've Read

Important ideas
1. What is space and where does it start?

_____

_____

2. Traveling from the Earth, what is the closest body to Earth that you will meet in space?

_____

_____

3. What are the parts of our solar system?

_____

_____

4. How is being on the moon different from being on the Earth?

_____

_____

Use what you've learned before
5. The moon keeps its orbit around the Earth because of the Earth's gravity. What do you think keeps the Earth in orbit around the sun?

_____

Important word meanings

Find these words in the article: *atmosphere, satellite, orbit,* and *solar system.* Circle each one where you find it. Write down the meaning of each word or phrase in the margin next to it. Then use each one in a sentence that tells something about exploring space.

_____

_____

_____

_____

Using skills and strategies

You can make a semantic map to organize ideas or words. Work with a group to fill in words or phrases to fit the three topics. For example, under *problems in space*, you can write *bring own air*. Add other topics if you wish. Doing the map will help you organize what you have learned in the article.

Space

traveling to space	problems in space	bodies in space
_____	_____	_____
_____	_____	_____
_____	_____	_____

Writing

On a separate sheet of paper, make two lists of the things you would take on a trip to the moon. Make one list *Things I Need to Have.* Make the other *Things I Would Like to Have.* Share your lists with others in your class.

Your important ideas

Look back over the article. Write down one idea that seems to be the most important one to you—the one idea that you would like to remember.

_____

_____

Your important words

Look back at the words you have learned as you read about space. Write down the word or words that you think are most important—that you would like to remember.

_____

_____

Why People Will Live and Work in Space

What do you already know?

Write down three facts that you already know about how or why people will live and work in space. Work with a partner, if you like.

1. _____

2. _____

3. _____

Make predictions

Look at the pictures and read the headings. Then write down three facts that you think you will learn as you read this article.

1. _____

2. _____

3. _____

Set your purpose for reading

Write down one thing you hope to find out about living and working in space as you read this article.

_____

_____

Learn important words

Study the meanings of the words below and how they are used in sentences. Knowing these words might help you as you read this article.

solar energy—energy given off by the sun. *Solar energy is used to heat all the city buildings.*

spacecraft—anything that is designed to fly in space. *Some spacecraft carry people and special cameras.*

dock—to join while in space. *The spacecraft will dock with the space station that is orbiting the Earth.*

People started moving to the West in the 1800s. They called the West the frontier because it was strange and new and sometimes dangerous. People went to the frontier because there was gold that could make them rich. There also was cheap land that people could farm.

Some people today look at space as our new frontier. Like the West, living in space would be a dangerous venture. But people see good reasons to go, too.

Gathering the sun's energy

On Earth people burn fuels such as coal, natural gas, and oil. One reason for burning these fuels is to make electricity. Because we need a lot of electricity to cool us and to make goods, we use a lot of fuel. We use so much fuel that we are running out.

Using skills and strategies

Cause-effect relationships

Many articles tell you what happens and why. *What happens* is an effect. *Why it happens* is a cause. Words such as *because, so,* and *since* give you clues about what happens and why. For example, you have just read that we are running out of certain fuels. Running out of these fuels is an effect. Why are we running out of these fuels? Look for the sentence that begins with the clue word *because*. Circle this sentence. It tells you why.

You may know that we can also make electricity from the sun. The sun gives off solar energy. The large, flat panels on the house in the picture collect solar energy and change it to electricity. The energy then heats and cools the house.

This building is heated and cooled by solar energy. The flat solar panels on the side of the house collect the energy and turn it into electricity.

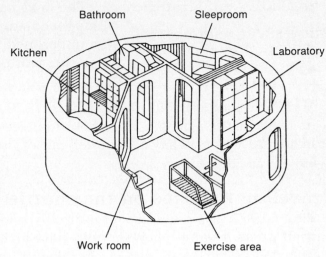

Bathroom   Sleeproom

Kitchen   Laboratory

Work room   Exercise area

Solar energy could replace coal, gas, and oil. However, before we can use solar energy in such large amounts, we need to be able to collect more of it. The atmosphere keeps much solar energy from reaching the Earth. So we could collect more solar energy if the collectors were outside the atmosphere.

The job of building solar collectors could be done in space. Getting energy from the sun would give people on Earth all the energy they would need for a long, long time.

Learning about the planets

People living in space could also help us learn more about the planets. Since the planets are so far away, spacecraft now can't get there and back. But people living in space could work at pit stops in space! In that way, we could go farther and farther out into space.

Skylab—our first space station

Skylab was a space station put into orbit around the Earth in 1973. *Skylab* proved that people could live and work in space. People flew to *Skylab* in a spacecraft powered by a rocket. The spacecraft docked with *Skylab*. The people then left the spacecraft and went into the space station. Three groups of people went to *Skylab* in 1973 and 1974. They studied the stars, the sun, and the atmosphere.

We learned two very important things on *Skylab*. First, people can live in space for a long time. Second, people can solve problems in space. We learned about problems when *Skylab* was damaged during its take-off from Earth. The first group of people who worked on *Skylab* fixed the damage while the space station orbited the Earth. These people showed that living and working in space is possible, even when things don't go as planned.

Using skills and strategies

Cause-effect relationships

The next paragraph describes an effect—what happened—and tells why it happened—the cause. The effect is underlined for you. Circle the cause. Remember to look for clue words that will help you.

Skylab no longer orbits the Earth. In 1979, *Skylab* fell out of its orbit. It then blew apart when it entered the Earth's atmosphere. Experts say *Skylab* fell out of its orbit because of storms on the sun.

Traveling to space on the shuttle

Before 1981, we used a spacecraft only once because it burned up as it came back through the Earth's atmosphere. We needed a spacecraft that could take off like a rocket but land like an airplane.

On April 12, 1981, the first space shuttle went into space. The shuttle can carry people and big loads. It can be used again and again. In 1983, a shuttle carried a space station called *Spacelab* into space. The space station was put into orbit and the shuttle came back to Earth. The shuttle will make the building of space stations easier and cheaper. It makes the idea of living and working in space more possible.

Think About What You've Read

Important ideas

1. What are two jobs people could do in space?

_____

_____

2. Why do people want to use more solar energy than they use now?

_____

_____

3. How will the shuttle make living on a space station more possible?

_____

_____

Use what you've learned before

4. What do you think might be some of the dangers of living on a space station that is orbiting the Earth?

_____

_____

Important word meanings

Choose words from the list to complete the sentences.
You will not use one of the words.

solar energy   atmosphere   gravity
dock   spacecraft   orbit

1. The moon moves around Earth because of a force called _____ .

2. An _____ is the path the Earth follows around the sun.

3. Earth's _____ keeps some of the sun's energy from reaching Earth.

4. The space shuttle is a _____ that can be used again.

5. A source of power we get from the sun is _____ .

Using skills and strategies

You have learned to look for causes that explain effects as
you read. Complete the following cause-effect sentence
pairs. When you are finished, share your ideas with others.

cause: _____

effect: People need to find fuels that will not get used up.

cause: We needed a spacecraft that could land like an airplane.

effect: _____

Writing

You are a reporter. You have been sent to interview the
first people coming home from living on a space station.
You can ask them five questions. On a separate paper, write
the questions you would ask. Do not write questions they
would answer *yes* or *no*. Ask questions that would give you
information on what it was like to live on a space station.

Your important ideas

Look back over the article. Write down one idea that
seems to be the most important one to you—the one idea
that you would like to remember.

_____

_____

Your important words

Look back at the words you learned as you read about
living and working in space. Write down the word or words
that are most important—that you would like to remember.

_____

_____

Astronaut Flight Training

What do you already know?

Write down three facts that you already know about astronauts or flight. Work with a partner, if you like.

1. _____

2. _____

3. _____

Make predictions

Quickly skim the article and notice some of the first lines of the letter. Also look at the pictures. Then write down three facts that you think you will learn as you read this article.

1. _____

2. _____

3. _____

Set your purpose for reading

Write down one thing you hope to find out about astronaut flight training as you read this article.

_____

_____

Learn important words

Study the meanings of the words below and how they are used in sentences. Knowing these words might help you as you read this article.

astronaut—a pilot or a member of the crew of a spacecraft. *An astronaut learns how to dock at a space station.*

military—having to do with the armed forces. *Military pilots include men and women from the navy and air force.*

simulator—a machine that creates the effects of an actual event. *The simulator gave the feelings of a rocket takeoff.*

In May, 1961, Alan Shepard became the first American in space. Inside his spacecraft, Shepard flew 116 miles over Earth and then fell back down into the sea. After this flight, President John Kennedy said that the United States should send people to the moon and back. Americans worked hard to do this. Success came in July, 1969. Neil Armstrong and Edwin Aldrin became the first to set foot on the moon.

The first astronauts went to school to learn about space. All were military test pilots with more than 1,000 hours of flying experience. However, they had much to learn before they could be astronauts. For example, they learned how to survive in different kinds of places. They also learned what it feels like to be blasted into and out of space.

Using skills and strategies

Main idea and details

The most important idea in a paragraph is its main idea. Sometimes, a single sentence states the main idea. The main idea in the paragraph you just read is underlined. Details that add to the main idea are usually found in the same paragraph. The paragraph contains many details about the first astronauts and the school they attended. Circle two of these details.

As you read the letter from the astronaut below, write down one important detail for each paragraph. Use the margin to write your answers.

Johnson Space Center
Houston, Texas

Dear Mom,

When I said I wanted to be an astronaut, I never thought I'd have to go through torture! I'll tell you all about what we've been doing. The way I see it, if a person can live through the training, going to outer space will be easy.

We started out in a classroom. It was just like any other school. We learned about the solar system, how planes and rockets fly, and all about weather. We learned what people already know about going to and from space.

Many astronauts were test pilots who flew planes like this one.

Astronauts learn how it feels to be weightless in space. Padded aircraft are used to protect the astronauts.

The other people in the class are really smart. (I sent a picture of some of them.) All of them have college degrees. Most of them learned to fly in the military, just like I did.

Mom, the classroom work was hard. I studied after class and every night. But it wasn't as hard as what came next—the survival training! Half-way through, I wondered if we were training to go to space or making a Tarzan movie.

From the classroom, we went to a jungle in Panama. Here we learned how to survive if our spacecraft landed in a jungle. They took us into the jungle by helicopter and left us there in groups of two for three days. We learned how to find food in the jungle. We caught and ate bats, wild pigs, hairless caterpillars, and termites.

From Panama we went to a desert. After all, our spacecraft might land in a desert, not a jungle. I think the desert was worse. The sand was 148 degrees. All we wanted was water. Shade ran a close second! Did you know that you can live for weeks in the desert as long as you have water? Without it, you die in a few days. In the desert we learned how far a little water can take you.

When we got back to Houston, they said the rest of the training would be like a day at a fair. I thought it would be fun. I was wrong. The simulator wasn't fun. The simulator showed us if our bodies could take it in space.

First they put us inside ovens heated to 140 degrees. Then they put us into an ice pack to see what would happen. They did this because the temperatures are freezing and boiling in space. You've got to be able to stand the changes if they happen.

Next they hung us upside down and put us in airplanes with padded walls. This was to help us know what it feels like to be weightless. You know, there's no gravity in space.

Mom, remember when we went to the fair when I was ten? We went on the ride where you stand against a wall in a round room. Remember what happens next? The room starts spinning faster and faster, and then the floor drops out. But you don't fall. You're pressed up against the wall.

Well, that ride is like a machine they put us into next. It's called a centrifuge. When you blast off from Earth, your spacecraft speeds up. It speeds up so quickly that people on board are pushed in their seats with unusual force.

The force that pushes people back against the seats in a spacecraft is measured in a unit called "g's." A person begins to feel uncomfortable at 8 g's. You have trouble breathing at 10 g's. The centrifuge tested us at 15 g's. This means that my 165-pound body was pressed against the seat with a force of about 2,500 pounds. I felt like I weighed a ton for hours after getting off.

We used other simulators to practice flying and guiding the spacecraft. We learned what we would do while we were in space.

I'll be home in another month or two. If I pass all the tests, I might be chosen to go on the next flight to space. Maybe I'll get to the moon. If I do, Mom, you'll have to wait until I get home to hear all about it. As far as I know, they're not delivering mail from there yet.

Love,
B. J.

Think About What You've Read

Important ideas

1. Who was the first American in space?

_____

2. What are the three areas of training that an astronaut goes through?

_____

_____

3. Why do astronauts go through survival training?

_____

_____

Use what you've learned before

4. Why would an astronaut practice under water in a diving suit?

_____

_____

Important word meanings

Use your own words to write a meaning for each word below. Then write a sentence using each word.

astronaut— _____

_____

military— _____

_____

spacecraft— _____

_____

Using skills and strategies

Look back at the details you wrote in the margin about the astronauts' training. Write down four details that you think are most important on the lines below.

_____

_____

_____

_____

Writing

Use the details you wrote down above. On a separate sheet of paper, write two paragraphs that tell how astronauts are trained. Make sure each paragraph has a main idea.

Your important ideas

Look back over the article. Write down one idea that seems to be the most important one to you—the one idea that you would like to remember.

_____

_____

Your important words

Look back at the words you have learned as you read about astronaut flight training. Write down the word or words that you think are most important—that you would like to remember.

_____

_____

_____

Did a Death Star Kill the Dinosaurs?

What do you already know?

Write down three facts that you already know about dinosaurs. Work with a partner, if you like.

1. _____

2. _____

3. _____

Make predictions

Look at the pictures and read the headings. Then skim the first sentences of the paragraphs. Write down three ideas that you think you will learn as you read this article.

1. _____

2. _____

3. _____

Set your purpose for reading

Write down one thing you hope to find out about the death of the dinosaurs as you read this article.

_____

_____

Learn important words

Study the meanings of the words below and how they are used in sentences. Knowing these words might help you as you read this article.

extinct—no longer on the Earth. *Dinosaurs are extinct.*

fossil—an outline or the hardened remains of a living thing. *The rock contained a fossil.*

comet—a bright body in space with a starlike center and a tail that orbits the sun. *A comet has an egg-shaped orbit.*

Millions of years ago, dinosaurs like the ones in the picture lived on the Earth. Dinosaurs were great and wonderful reptiles. Today young people and adults alike wonder about them. We wonder what they really looked like. We wonder how they moved. We wonder how they fought. Mostly we wonder: What happened to them? Why aren't they around today?

About 65 million years ago, something happened that made the dinosaurs extinct. In fact, this event killed about one-half or three-fourths of all living things on the Earth.

Scientists have had many ideas over the years to explain why the dinosaurs and other forms of life became extinct. One of these ideas says that 65 million years ago, something crashed into the Earth. The crash sent so much dust into the atmosphere that the sun was blocked. No sunlight reached the Earth for months. As a result, plants died. Animals that ate plants died. Animals that ate other animals also died.

Using skills and strategies

Clarifying

You often come to ideas or words you don't understand as you read an article. You then need to clarify, or figure out, the ideas or words. For example, you might not know what *atmosphere* means. You can clarify its meaning in different ways. You could look the word up in a dictionary. You could think how it is used in the paragraph. You can also clarify by remembering how the word was used in other articles. These are called clarifying strategies.

As you read this article, circle any words you need to clarify. Then choose a clarifying strategy that will help you find the meaning of the word. When you finish, write the definition of the word in the margin. Write down the way you clarified its meaning under the definition.

Scientists find a clue in a rock

In 1978, a scientist found a rock that was 65 million years old. Trapped in the rock were many small fossils of animals that lived in the sea at that time. But the fossils were all in the bottom part of the rock. All the other living things had died before the top part of the rock was formed. The scientist later found that these plants and animals died at the same time dinosaurs became extinct.

More scientists studied the rock. The rock had a lot of a material called iridium in it. This was unusual because the material isn't often found in rocks. Scientists do know that iridium falls to the Earth when tiny meteors fall apart coming into our atmosphere.

Could comets kill things on Earth?

Scientists began to think that something from space caused the dinosaurs and other living things to die out. They studied more fossils. They discovered that there were other periods in the Earth's history when many plants and animals had died out. These periods took place 26 to 28 million years apart. Scientists began to think that some regular event caused the destruction. This would explain the regular pattern of extinctions.

The Orbit of the Death Star

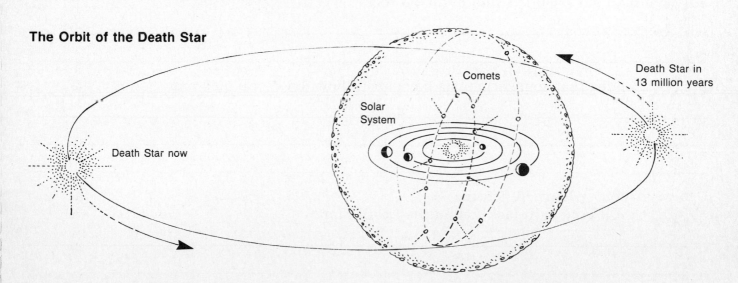

Death Star now

Death Star in 13 million years

Comets

Solar System

Some scientists thought a comet might be the cause. A comet looks like a fuzzy star with a long tail. Comets orbit the sun. We have seen a few comets, but most travel too far from the Earth to be seen.

After much thinking and studying, scientists have an idea of what happens every 26 to 28 million years. The drawing at the bottom of page 139 helps explain the idea. The idea involves comets and the sun.

Scientists think that the sun has a twin! This star—sometimes called Nemesis and sometimes called the Death Star—moves around the sun. Every 26 to 28 million years, the Death Star comes near a group of comets. The Death Star changes the comets' orbits. One or more of the comets then crashes into the Earth. Enough dust gets thrown up that the sun's energy is blocked. Life on the Earth either freezes or starves to death.

The idea of the Death Star has not been proved. In fact, scientists have not yet found the Death Star. However, if the sun does have a twin, we should be able to find it. Then we can learn its orbit. We can figure out where it was 65 million years ago. We also can start to get ready for the next time the Death Star is in the same position—about 13 million years from now.

Think About What You've Read

Important ideas

1. What do people want to know most about the dinosaurs?

_____

2. What clue did scientists find in an old rock?

_____

_____

3. Tell the idea that some scientists have about how dinosaurs died out.

_____

_____

_____

Use what you've learned before
4. Why is it a very hard task to find the Death Star?

_____

_____

Using skills and strategies

Each of the words below was used in this article. Write the meaning of each word. Then tell how you went about finding the word's meaning.

1. What is the meaning of *fossil*? How did you find its meaning?

_____

_____

2. What is the meaning of *iridium*? How did you find its meaning?

_____

_____

3. What is the meaning of *comet*? How did you find its meaning?

_____

_____

4. What is the meaning of *extinct*? How did you find its meaning?

_____

_____

Writing

Pretend you are the one to discover the Death Star. Write a headline and the first paragraph for a newspaper article telling about your discovery. Your headline should be exciting. Your paragraph should tell what you discovered, how you discovered it, and why the discovery is important. Make up any information you need for your paragraph. Do your writing on another piece of paper. Share it with others in your class.

Your important ideas

Look back over the article. Write down one idea that seems to be the most important one to you—the one idea that you would like to remember.

_____

_____

Your important words

Look back at the words you have learned as you read about the Death Star. Write down the word or words that you think are most important—that you would like to remember.

_____

_____

Reviewing what you have learned

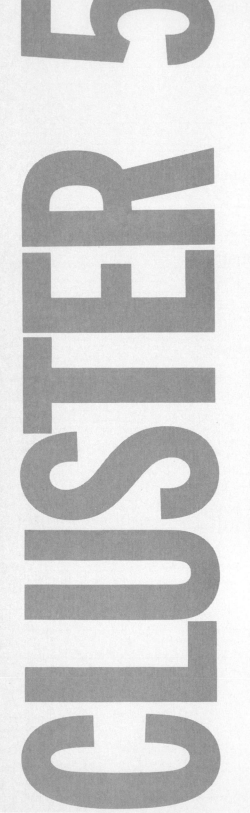

Some facts and ideas you have learned

You learned many important facts and ideas as you read about space. A few of them are listed below. Add your own important ideas to the end of this list. You can look back to the "Your important ideas" section of each lesson to remember the ideas you wrote down.

- Space starts about 100 miles above the Earth.
- People lived and worked in *Skylab* for a long time and safely returned to Earth.
- Astronauts learn how to survive if their spacecraft falls to Earth and lands in a desert or a jungle.
- Some scientists think a Death Star caused comets to crash to the Earth, killing the dinosaurs.

_____

_____

_____

_____

Some word meanings you have learned

Here are some of the important words you learned in the articles you read. Make sure you understand their meanings. Then add important words of your own. You can look back at the "Your important words" section of each lesson to remember the words you wrote down.

spacecraft—anything designed to fly in space. *The spacecraft docked with the space station.*

orbit—the path of a body in space around another. *The moon orbits the Earth.*

extinct—no longer on the Earth. *Dinosaurs are extinct.*

_____

_____

_____

Purposes for reading

Look back at the section at the beginning of every lesson called "Set your purpose for reading." Did your purposes help you discover information? Write down one purpose and tell how it helped you in your reading.

_____

_____

Writing: letters

You learned many facts and ideas about space and how it affects the lives of people on the Earth. Do you think the United States government should try to learn more about space? Or do you think our government should spend that time and money solving the problems on the Earth? Maybe you think our government should do both. Write a letter to the President stating your ideas.

Using skills and strategies

Look back at the letter you wrote. Does each paragraph in your letter have a main idea? On the lines below, write a list of your main ideas. In your letter, did you include details that add information to each main idea? If not, write the letter again, making sure that you organize your ideas carefully.

Revising

Read your letter aloud to a friend. Are your ideas clear? Change your letter if you need to. Mail your letter to the President. If you receive a reply, share it with your class.

Activities

1. You can feel what it's like to work in a place where you are weightless. The next time you are in a swimming pool, hold your breath and try to do something, such as tying a knot under water. Floating in the water is like floating in space. Don't try this unless you are a good swimmer.

2. Use different-sized balls to get an idea of the sizes of the moon and the Earth. Use a tennis ball for the moon and a basketball for the Earth. Find out how the moon orbits the Earth and move the balls to show it.

3. You may have heard of the space shuttle *Challenger*. It blew up in a terrible accident in 1986. Go to the library and find some information about the *Challenger*. Report to your class about what happened.

4. The picture shows a telescope used a long time ago to look at the objects in the sky. If you can, visit a planetarium and find out what kinds of telescopes are used to study the sky today.

5. Look in a book on dinosaurs and find out what animal alive today is most like the dinosaurs that lived 65 million years ago. Write a short report about the animal.

ACKNOWLEDGMENTS

Photo Credits

Cluster 1: 5: Bruce Coleman Inc/Kim Taylor. **18:** UPI/Bettmann Newsphotos. **19:** Bruce Coleman Inc/M. Timothy O'Keefe. **23:** The Bettmann Archive. **24**(left): ©Bohdan Hrynewych/Stock Boston. **24**(right): Bruce Coleman Inc/Lee Foster. **29:** Courtesy of NASA.

Cluster 2: 35: Bruce Coleman Inc/Giorgio Gualco. **37:** Dallas and John Heaton/Click/Chicago. **44**(left): Bruce Coleman Inc/Andrew Rakoczy. **44**(middle): Bruce Coleman Inc/Joe McDonald. **44**(right): Animals Animals/©L.L. Rue III. **45:** Bruce Coleman Inc/Giorgio Gualco. **49:** AP/Wide World Photos. **50:** UPI/Bettmann Newsphotos. **55:** Bruce Coleman Inc/Giorgio Gualco. **61:** Bruce Coleman Inc/George Rockwill.

Cluster 3: 67: ©Gabor Demjen/Stock Boston. **69:** R. Piddington/Black Star. **71:** Bruce Coleman Inc/Nicholas Devore III. **75:** ©Fredrik D. Bodin/Stock Boston. **80**(left): ©Jeff Albertson/Stock Boston. **80:**(right): ©Joseph Schuyler/Stock Boston. **81**(top): ©Owen Franken/Stock Boston. **81:**(bottom left): ©Patrice Flesch/Stock Boston. **81**(bottom right): ©Gale Zucker/Stock Boston. **85**(top): Steve Schapiro/Gamma-Liaison. **85**(bottom): Bonnie Schiffman/Gamma-Liaison. **86:** ©Mike Mazzaschi/Stock Boston.

Clsuter 4: 91: Susan Malis/MGA Chicago. **93:** ©Elizabeth Crews/Stock Boston. **94:** Code of laws of the Babylonian king, Hammurabi, reigned from 2067-2025 B.C. The Bettmann Archive. **95:** Signing of the Constitution, 1787, by Howard Chandler Christy. Historical Pictures Service, Chicago. **100-102:** Courtesy of the Illinois YMCA Youth & Government Program. **112:** Woodcut from the Bettmann Archive. **113:** The Bettmann Archive. **114:** Painting by Louis Schultze. Missouri Historical Society. The Bettmann Archive. **115:** The Bettmann Archive.

Cluster 5: 121: Courtesy of NASA. **124:** Courtesy of NASA. **128:** Photri/MGA Chicago. **129:** Courtesy of NASA. **133:** Photri/MGA Chicago. **134:** Courtesy of NASA.

Illustrators

Sharon Elzaurdia; Masheris Associates/Donald Charles; Susan C. Mills; Jack Wallen; John Walter & Assoc./Jack Wallen, John Walter, Jr.